MARLENE DIETRICH

MARLENE DIETRICH

A Pyramid Illustrated History of the Movies

by
CHARLES SILVER

General Editor: **TED SENNETT**

PUBLICATIONS
NEW YORK

PN2658
.D5S5
c1

For Mama and MOMA
Karen and Marlene
and in memory of Dad and Jo

MARLENE DIETRICH
A Pyramid Illustrated History of the Movies

ISBN 0-515-03484-3

Library of Congress Catalog Card Number: 74-9336

Pyramid Edition published October 1974

Printed in the United States of America

Pyramid Books are published by Pyramid Communications, Inc. Its trademarks, consisting of the word "Pyramid" and the portrayal of a pyramid, are registered in the United States Patent Office.

Pyramid Communications, Inc.
919 Third Avenue, New York, N.Y. 10022

CONDITIONS OF SALE

graphic design by anthony basile

ACKNOWLEDGMENTS

When one completes a first book, it is possible there is a tendency to thank too many people, since the knowledge of how long the first one took makes the prospect of a second one all the more dubious. If I appear too grateful, therefore, I crave your indulgence.

Both Andrew Sarris and Herman G. Weinberg published their first books on Josef von Sternberg and more than peripherally, therefore, on Ms. Dietrich. I, like anyone else who aspires to write seriously on American films, am in considerable debt to these two men, and if this book can be construed by them as being within the tradition they have established, I would be honored.

On a more personal level I am extremely grateful for the opportunity given me to write by mentors such as Eileen Bowser and Adrienne Mancia, Curators of Film at the Museum of Modern Art, Richard Corliss, Editor of *Film Comment,* and Ted Sennett.

Special thanks is due my colleagues in the Museum of Modern Art Department of Film for their patient cooperation with this project. Stephen Harvey, Mary Corliss, Arthur Steiger, Emily Sieger, Jon Gartenberg, Mark Power, and Robert Regan have been particularly generous.

For support and encouragement of varying kinds, I must mention Harry Sitren, Albert and Hortense Green, Robert and Lillian Fraker, Clyde Norton, Howard Mandelbaum, and James Tamulis.

Assistance in viewing films has come from Patrick Sheehan and Paul Spehr of the Library of Congress Motion Picture Section, Dave Kehr of Doc Films, Doug Lemza of Films Incorporated, Robert Baumstone of Institutional Cinema Service, and Mike Stephens of Westinghouse Broadcasting. Most of the photographs are from the superb collection of Jerry Vermilye; others are from Cinemabilia and Movie Star News.

Finally, my greatest debt is to someone deserving of the kind of litany Marlene recites when she introduces Burt Bacharach: my teacher, my arranger, my conductor, etc. For thousands of hours of perceptively stimulating and witty conversation, even when he was only playing Melvyn Douglas to my Herbert Marshall, I want to thank my good friend, Michael Kerbel.
                                                            —Charles Silver

P.1167-

CONTENTS

WEIMARLENE

His name was Josef von Sternberg. He was from Vienna by way of Brooklyn, Fort Lee, and Hollywood. He had come to Berlin to direct the first German talkie, a film financed by the same man who was soon to finance Adolf Hitler. The year was 1929 and the movie was *The Blue Angel*.

Sternberg, in his autobiography, *Fun in a Chinese Laundry* (Macmillan, 1965), describes Berlin as a seething ocean of inflated currency and confused values where "morality became a curiosity." He was there at the request of Emil Jannings, the genius of expressionist acting and the reigning star of the German cinema. Jannings, during his brief sojourn in America, had been directed by Sternberg in *The Last Command*, the story of a Czarist general turned Hollywood extra—who dies portraying a Czarist general. Following this exposure to the actor's infantile temper tantrums, the director had informed Jannings that he would never direct him again if he were the last actor on earth. Sternberg attributes his change of heart to his being touched by Jannings' request. UFA, the dominant production company in the German cinema, had offered their star the choice of any director in the world. Emil chose his old "friend" Jo or Julius, as Jannings insisted on calling him,

and Julius came to do battle with the primitive sound equipment and a three-hundred-pound, sausage-devouring actor who "behaved as if we were married."

The original conception of Jannings and producer Erich Pommer had been a film based on the life of Rasputin, of which there had been a German silent version the year before. Sternberg squelched that, and suggested an adaptation of Heinrich (brother of Thomas) Mann's 1905 novel, *Professor Unrat*. Rosa Fröhlich, the cabaret singer of the novel, was to be changed to Lola-Lola, a derivative of Wedekind's Lulu. Sternberg and his associates began to turn the Weimar Republic inside out in the search for Lola-Lola.

As Sternberg rejected all suggested candidates, he reports a rumor began to circulate that the woman he wanted did not exist. At one point he had looked at an uninteresting photograph of an actress described to him as "not at all bad from the rear, but do we not also need a face?" Her name was Marlene Dietrich, and she was appearing in Georg Kaiser's play *Zwei Krawatten* (Two Ties) along with Hans Albers and Rosa Valetti, both already cast for *The Blue Angel*. As Sternberg describes her, Dietrich's appearance was ideal for Lola-Lola; she was a woman over whom Toulouse-Lautrec would have turned handsprings. Despite the protests of all concerned, Sternberg asked Dietrich to come to his office. The director got rid of Jannings' complaining presence by sending the star on the errand of sampling every sausage in Germany at his expense. Dietrich treated the prospect of starring in *The Blue Angel* with the same disdain she was later to offer the men in several other Sternberg films. She was a creature of lethargy whose previous life and career had, as Sternberg describes her, left her with a feeling of little worth. She had already been "discovered" many times before.

Dietrich's mentor, director Josef von Sternberg

* * * * *

Maria Magdalene Dietrich was born on December 27 sometime after the turn of the century. The place was probably either Weimar or Berlin, but since her myth has for so long submerged her mortality, the exact time and place can matter only to pedants. Both her father, who died when she was a child, and her stepfather, Herr von Losch, were military men. Losch was killed on the Russian front during World War I, and Uncle Max Dietrich's zeppelin was shot down while re-turning from a bombing mission over England. An auspicious career as a violinist was curtailed by a wrist injury, and a disappointed Marlene was forced to seek less reputable employment as an actress.

Her involvement with the celebrated Max Reinhardt's theater school is a matter of some dispute. Dietrich's frequently detailed descriptions of her training with the maestro would carry more conviction if they were not coupled with her denials of having appeared in the dozen and a half films she made before *The Blue Angel*. Sternberg reports that Reinhardt's eyebrows were raised for a full twenty minutes after Marlene informed him of their previous relationship. In any event, it was not unusual for Reinhardt's students to be involved

11

in Berlin's thriving film industry, and, one way or another, the young girl drifted into movies.

A letter in the files of the Museum of Modern Art reports an incident during the shooting in 1922 of *Der Kampf Um's Ich* (The Struggle For One's Soul). The letter was written by the cameraman on the film, Stefan Lorant, later an historian in the United States. It tells of a young girl coming to the Tempelhof Studio on a hot day with a note from the head of the studio asking Lorant to make a test of her. It had been a frustrating day of work on a film with which the participants were unhappy. The girl was subjected to insensitive horseplay and teasing. She was finally asked to act out various emotions for the test. "I remember seeing the test," Lorant writes, "and it was terrible. Yet this was the first film test of Marlene."

After a small part in a film called *Der Kleine Napoleon* (1923), Dietrich had a fairly substantial role in an Emil Jannings vehicle, *The Tragedy of Love* (1923), directed by Joe May who later came to Hollywood. She played a peasant girl in *Man By the Roadside* (1923) which starred and was directed by Wilhelm (later William) Dieterle. (Some twenty years later Dietrich was to appear in his Arabian Nights fantasy, *Kismet*.) There followed *The Leap Into Life* (1924) and then, her first "important" film in retrospect, Pabst's *Joyless Street* (1925).

THE BLUE ANGEL (1929). With Emil Jannings

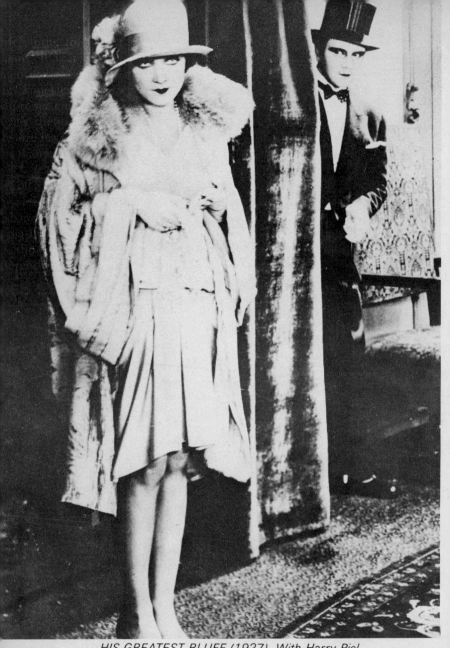

HIS GREATEST BLUFF (1927). With Harry Piel

Joyless Street is an exploration of postwar poverty and decadence in Vienna. Its star, Asta Nielsen, could hardly have been aware that she was appearing with two women who would shortly eclipse her substantial reputation—Greta Garbo and Marlene Dietrich. Garbo has the second female lead, and if her performance does not show clearly why she was soon to be brought to Hollywood and stardom, she is not the only one in the film who reflects Pabst's limited talent with actors.

Dietrich appears on the line perennially waiting outside the shop of butcher Werner Krauss. Pabst crosscuts this symbol of poverty with scenes of the corrupt nightlife of gay Vienna. There is actually a shot of Nielsen, Garbo, and Dietrich, and when Garbo faints from hunger, Dietrich comforts her. Watching Garbo being helped away by the police, Marlene brushes her hair out of her eyes and drags her fingers lightly across her face in a characteristic gesture which was to appear in many of her later films.

As the line breaks up in the morning with no meat available, Dietrich befriends Nielsen. They walk together to the outside of a dress shop (the cardboard set moves as Nielsen leans against it) and observe the butcher giving his meat to a pair of tarts. Later in the film Dietrich appears again with Nielsen and walks toward the camera, hand on hip in the best Marlene manner. Now in closeup, she again makes the gesture of brushing her hair aside, lights a cigarette, and upstages Nielsen by blowing smoke in her face—all vintage Dietrich. Finally, it is Marlene who, in a fit of rage, kills the butcher for his cruelty and is pursued down the street by his dog in a long expressionistic tracking shot. Her performance, although brief, is very effective and belies any suggestion that Sternberg taught her everything she knows.

Dietrich's first UFA film was *Manon Lescaut* (1926), a lavish costume drama directed by Arthur Robison, well known for his earlier *Warning Shadows*. It starred Lya de Putti who had played opposite Jannings in Dupont's famous *Variety*. This was followed by a role as a coquette in Alexander Korda's *A Modern Du Barry* (1926). Marlene also appeared as a dress extra in Korda's *Madame Doesn't Want Children* (1926). (A decade later she was to star in Korda's *Knight Without Armour* in England.) Then came two films directed by Dr. Willi Wolff—*Heads Up, Charly!* (1926) and *The Imaginary Baron* (1927). The second of these, a comedy, gave Marlene her largest role to date. The star, Reinhold Schünzel, was to be reunited with her in 1947 in *Golden Earrings*. Another comedy with the popular Harry Piel,

I KISS YOUR HAND, MADAME (1929). With Harry Liedtke

His Greatest Bluff (1927), marked the end of the first stage of Dietrich's screen career.

In the course of her acting pursuits, Marlene had met and married a young Austrian production assistant, Rudolf Sieber. They had a daughter, Maria, in 1925, who, under her married name, Riva, was to become a dramatic star on American television a quarter of a century later. In addition to these familial activities, Marlene appeared on the stage. In 1927 in Vienna, she did *Broadway* with Willi Forst, and, while there, they appeared together in the film, *Café Electric*. It was a leading role, and she received good reviews. With each new film (*Princess Olala*, *I Kiss Your Hand, Madame*, *The Woman One Longs For*, *The Ship of Lost Souls*), she became more glamorous and more prominent. In the last of these four, directed by Maurice Tourneur who had been a major Hollywood director in the twenties, Dietrich wore men's clothing in most scenes. She was reunited with Forst for *Dangers of the Engagement Period*, her final film before Sternberg "discovered" her.

* * * * *

"Miss Dietrich is me—I am Miss Dietrich." These are Sternberg's words expressed in a fragmentary interview with Peter Bogdanovich (*Movie*, #13). To penetrate to the core of such a comment is clearly beyond the scope of this book, and

16

one might speculate that the enigma of their relationship is probably as multi-layered as an onion the size of Emil Jannings. It is sufficient to say that with the unpopular selection of Marlene to play Lola-Lola, Sternberg and Dietrich embarked upon one of the most complex and probably the most artistically productive liaison in the history of the cinema. The beginning, however, fraught with threats from a jealous Jannings and reluctance on the part of Dietrich herself, was less than auspicious.

Sternberg's problems with *The Blue Angel* were compounded by the excessively primitive nature of the untried German sound equipment and by a male star determined to demonstrate his mastery of German by embellishing the script "with archaic inflections that had not been heard since the Middle Ages." Sternberg's unflagging efforts to combat this outrage are echoed in the film itself during the scene where Jannings corrects his student's recital of Hamlet's soliloquy. (Since the character of Professor Rath is derived from the director's childhood Hebrew teacher in Vienna, there are many reverberations, indeed, to the linguistics of *The Blue Angel*. Regretfully, I have never been able to

THE WOMAN ONE LONGS FOR (U.S.: THREE LOVES) (1929).
With Fritz Kortner

THE BLUE ANGEL (1929). With Emil Jannings

catch up with a print of the simultaneously produced English version of the film.)

We first experience Lola-Lola as her poster is doused by a scrubwoman, a dose of Sternbergian irony in the third shot of the film. (The opening shots are missing from most prints in commercial release at present in the United States.) The first five minutes establish a bird leitmotif (Jannings' pet canary dies; the landlady callously burns it; he looks askance at his breakfast egg, and later he is to transform himself

into a rooster amidst the cabaret birds just before his own death), and when we next see Dietrich she is on a signed postcard covered only in feathers which are made revelatory by Jannings' hot breath. It seems she distributes these cards to her admirers just as Dietrich herself was to do upon emerging from her dressing room during her first Broadway season in 1967. Her voice is heard over the postcards, and there is a fade to the live Lola-Lola with her hands characteristically on her hips, singing "Ich bin die fesche

Lola." She gives a blasé look around the sordid cabaret and then moves her eyes downward as she was to do in taking the measure of so many men in the years and films to come.

From the very first scenes he ever shot in *The Salvation Hunters*, Sternberg proved himself the master of milieu and atmosphere, crowding his films with a complexity of imagery and texture unequaled in all cinema. This skill was more than amply displayed in the creation of the ambience which was the Blue Angel cabaret, the perfect setting for Lola-Lola's moths to cluster around her flame. It is a world where the women come as cheaply as the beer, pigs' knuckles, and sauerkraut, the supreme embodiment of Sternberg's dictum that "the spell of the theatre has always been carnal rather than intellectual."

When Jannings comes off a classically expressionistic waterfront street and enters the cabaret ostensibly to reprimand Lola-Lola for corrupting his students, she is singing the song Helmut Berger was to

THE BLUE ANGEL (1929). With Hans Albers

THE BLUE ANGEL (1929). With Emil Jannings

parody in Luchino Visconti's *The Damned*. She is singing of her search for "einen richtigen Mann." ("Children, tonight, I look for someone real, a he-man, the right kind for me.") Before long she has turned her spotlight on the audience and has caught the bewildered Rath in its beam. It is only a short step to her dressing room and his enthrallment through such subtleties of her art as the dropping of her panties on his head. The second night when the professor returns to bring back the panties he had inadvertently carried away, he is further entwined by helping her with her mascara. As he bends down to pick up cigarettes from the floor, Jannings is confronted with the unsettling spectacle of Dietrich's exposed legs. Her quip, "Hey, professor, when you're finished, send me a postcard," unnerves him further.

These dressing room scenes are played with an innocent charm not seen in Jannings before or in Dietrich since. Lola-Lola is like no femme fatale the screen had yet witnessed. It is clear her intent is not to destroy Jannings, but rather to be amused by him as one might with an enormous Saint Bernard. When Jannings has an attack following the discovery of his students on the premises, Dietrich is sincerely concerned. When he defends her honor and her art, she is genuinely touched. And even when she does

flirt with him as he is seated in the celebrities' box and she sings "Falling in Love Again," there is a sense of conviction in her belief: "I know I'm not to blame . . . What am I to do? Can't help it."

The rest of *The Blue Angel* chronicles Professor Rath's descent to Professor Unrat (Garbage), and ultimately to death. From the initial break with his compulsive routine, the first fragmentary loss of dignity leads to a classically tragic destiny. This was the kind of role and performance which had made Jannings world famous (Sternberg's *The Last Command* was from the same mold), and Sternberg perceptively did not stray from the established form. In the preface to the published script to the film (Simon and Schuster, 1968), Sternberg comments on his actor: "To be humiliated was for him ecstasy." *The Blue Angel* must, therefore, have brought Jannings great joy. (His abasement here is more complete than anything he had suffered since Murnau's *The Last Laugh* [1924], which contends with *The Blue Angel* as the best film ever made in Germany.)

The Blue Angel looks very German and expressionistic. It is therefore atypical in many ways within the context of Sternberg's later career. The burst of madness which prompts Rath's gesture of proposal to Lola-Lola, however, is a fit of

Sternbergian romantic delirium to rival Dietrich's pursuit of Gary Cooper into the Moroccan desert. Thus, amidst his immersion in expressionism, Sternberg's characters still vent his own unique emotions, and one would not be surprised to hear the director argue with only minimal irony that four years with Lola-Lola was worth the price the professor pays. Sternberg himself spent five with Dietrich.

As Andrew Sarris has pointed out in *The Films of Josef von Sternberg* (The Museum of Modern Art, 1966), the ascent of Lola-Lola over the professor was paralleled in reality by Dietrich's triumph over Jannings. The actor must surely have sensed some of this during the production itself, and he spent considerable time pursuing Sternberg's affections which he fancied were being lavished on Dietrich. When it was all over, Jannings bid Sternberg a poignant farewell, saying that he knew that when either died, the other would shed a tear. For her part, Dietrich apparently persisted in telling her friends that the torture she was undergoing would ruin her, although the director met with very little resistance from her on the set.

Lola-Lola is a coarse and sketchy characterization, something less than a complete human being. The nuances of Dietrich's performance bridge the gaps; her total being is the product of gesture and mannerism. Much of what she is can be seen in Sternberg's silent films, personified by Georgia Hale, Evelyn Brent, and Betty Compson— women who straddle chairs, use their hands in a special way, have their souls revealed by the director's manipulation of light and shadow—women whose faces are, as he puts it, "treated like a landscape." Aside from her extraordinary beauty, Dietrich brought to this conception her ironic intelligence, a quality that women of 1929 were not encouraged to display. It was a short step from there to the perverse implications of pansexuality made more blatant with each Sternberg film. A contemporary writer has drawn an interesting parallel between Dietrich and Mick Jagger, artists whose persona are too rich and grandiose for the "normal" limitations imposed on human beings by an accident of birth. Whether the first symptom of a disease or the blossoming of a stronger breed, Lola-Lola is a beginning, and of the end, we have not yet had a full accounting.

FROM MOROCCO TO MAMOULIAN

The Blue Angel opened in Berlin on the eve of April Fool's Day 1930. Dietrich appeared on the stage of the Gloria Palast, and then sailed that very night for America and *Morocco*. Sternberg had long since departed, expecting never to see the actress again. In the bon voyage basket she had given him was a copy of Benno Vigny's novel *Amy Jolly*, a story Marlene labeled "weak lemonade." From this lemonade Sternberg drew his warmest and perhaps best film.

The early talkie was a slave to the microphone, enclosed as it was in a soundproof, immobile booth. Most filmmakers succumbed to the public fixation on dialogue, and paid little heed to the once-all-important visual quality of their films. A few directors like Alfred Hitchcock and Rouben Mamoulian dabbled in sound experimentation, achieving eccentric effects which at least relieved some of the tedium and suggested possibilities for the creative uses of sound. Around 1929 and 1930, directors like King Vidor, Ernst Lubitsch, and Howard Hawks in Hollywood and René Clair in France began to arrive at a successful melding of sound and image. Among his other contributions to films, Sternberg was the first director to attain full mastery and control over what was essentially a new medium. One of the key elements in this was his recognition of the value of silence. *Morocco* contains long sections sustained only by its stunning visual beauty overlaid with appropriate music and aural effects. (Significantly, the published script runs only forty-eight pages, as opposed to seventy-six for the shorter *Shanghai Express*.) Sternberg was the first artist to make an authentic virtue of the coming of sound.

The very complexity of the imagery of *The Blue Angel* and *Morocco*, its ability to retain fascination, was a positive factor in itself. Because of it Sternberg found less need to rely on musical numbers or on gimmickry like the clipped speech of Hawks' excellent *Dawn Patrol* (1930). Exotic locales such as North Africa provided greater opportunity for extraordinary visuals, and this doubtless did not discourage the director from choosing to drink Vigny's lemonade. From the first spectacular shots as the Foreign Legion marches into Mogador past bare-breasted natives and arrogant camels, it is evident that what is to follow is to be at the very least a dazzling display of stylistic imagination.

MOROCCO (1930). As Amy Jolly

.We are introduced to a veiled Amy Jolly (Dietrich) as her ship approaches a fog-ridden Mogador where she is to sing in a cabaret. In the scene which calls for Amy to tell fellow passenger Adolphe Menjou, "I won't need any help," there is no hint of the trauma experienced by all concerned on the first day of shooting in trying to get Marlene to shift gears into English, a strange new tongue for her. Sternberg's book recounts how this single line took the whole day to record, severely damaging his erstwhile reputation as one of Hollywood's fastest directors. We soon learn that Amy is a "suicide passenger" and Menjou "would be a great painter if he were not so rich." It is established that both are unfulfilled, thereby suggesting the possibility of a relationship. Their first meeting, however is less than auspicious.

When we next see her, it is a less sullen Dietrich. Significantly, she is in her dressing room where a good part of her life in Sternberg's films takes place. It is here that she prepares for the varying roles she must play. It is here she returns for shelter from the reality that always threatens to impinge on the cabaret theater from which she derives her sustenance. Dietrich has as her companions a black doll and an Oriental doll, refugees from her *Blue Angel* dressing room, soon to turn up again in *Dishonored* and *The Devil Is a Woman*. Later, when she agrees to marry Menjou, she hands him these dolls with the implication that this is the family he is adopting, the "children" which represent all that is of value in her existence to date. When Lo Tinto, the impresario, informs her before her performance that his cabaret is patronized by the finest society in Morocco, she demonstrates her contempt for conventional bourgeois values by popping her top hat, the hat which is momentarily to become the prime implement in the most daring reversal of sexual roles in the history of films.

As Dietrich performs "When Love Dies," climaxing in a famous kiss on a woman's mouth, she seems to be singing to both Menjou and Gary Cooper (Legionnaire Tom Brown), creating a triangular relationship which is to provide the film with its tension to the very last shot. Such an intangible commodity as dramatic tension is, like other abstractions, almost impossible to discuss adequately with mere words. Yet this is the stuff of Sternberg's narrative genius—the visualization of emotionally obsessive sexual relationships, embellished by milieu, and expressed through the subtle movement of the most intricate of human organs: eyes, mouths, hands, etc.

An extraordinary example is the scene in which Cooper comes to

Dietrich's apartment that first night after he has bought one of her "apples." Both expect a night of passion. Gradually, however, there is an emotional falling out, a need to deny one's needs, almost totally inexplicable in terms of the oblique dialogue. Eventually, Cooper reveals that he, too, is in effect, a suicide passenger, whose great regret is not having met Dietrich ten years ago. Both hint at great pain in their pasts, culminating in Amy's marvelous speech: "There's a Foreign Legion of women, too. But we have no uniforms—no flags —and no medals when we are brave . . . no wound stripes—when we are hurt." This prompts an offer of help from Cooper, and once again she must defend herself against the temptation of involvement: "No, I've heard that before." On paper the scene seems bland. On-screen, as Sternberg himself said in describing his art, "the very air becomes part of the effect."

A similarly expressive scene occurs in the office of the Legion Commandant (Ulrich Haupt). Cooper is under arrest for an incident involving an attempt to knife him by two Arabs in the employ of the commandant's wife (Eve South-

MOROCCO (1930). With Gary Cooper and Adolphe Menjou

MOROCCO (1930). With Adolphe Menjou

ern), the legionnaire's former mistress. Cooper refuses to implicate Southern, and Dietrich is called in for questioning. Menjou is also present. This complicated plot situation produces many emotional sparks. The tension is increased by Sternberg's attention to milieu —the feeling of great heat resulting from sunlight streaming in from all sides, Haupt's persistent use of a fan, and the disarray of the costumes.

Dietrich, away from her cabaret, seems uncomfortable. She attempts to remain nonchalant, fingering the window frame for dust, and finding it difficult to look any of the men in the eye. Much of the scene is played nonverbally, with long pauses heightening the tension.

After Cooper is taken away to jail, Menjou makes her another offer of help, this time for Cooper's sake. Dietrich asks his price, and Menjou blows the ashes from his cigarette before replying, "a smile." Dietrich grabs his arm affectionately and tells him, "I haven't got much more." This is her first sign of warmth toward him, and throughout their relationship, Menjou will settle for very little, remaining stoically good-natured even in the face of being deserted by Dietrich during the banquet commemorating their engagement later in the film. He will only smile and, without flinch-

27

MOROCCO (1930). With Gary Cooper

ing, explain to his guests, "You see, I love her. I'd do anything to make her happy."

Morocco has a directness about its characters' emotions in strong contrast with the ambiguity of some of the later Sternberg-Dietrich collaborations. Cooper's decision to change his mind and not desert the legion to run away with Amy takes place fully on screen. Dietrich leaves him in the dressing room to do her number ("Give Me the Man") after looking him up and down and staring intensely into his eyes. Sternberg shows Cooper trying on Dietrich's top hat and then putting his soldier's cap back on. No words are spoken, and there is little change of expression in Cooper's face. Yet it is established that he, like Jannings in *The Blue Angel*, cannot survive outside the profession and discipline with which he has defined himself for so long. Unlike Jannings, he is wise enough to

28

know that if he is to have Marlene, no matter how much he wants her, it must be on his own terms.

When Amy goes to see Cooper off the next morning, she can only stare at the Arab women who follow the men they love into the desert: "They must be mad." Her splendid drunk scene in the dressing room, concluding in her decision to marry Menjou, is a model of the expressiveness of Sternbergian gestures. As Amy throws her champagne at the mirror on which Cooper has scrawled his farewell message, she recoils and spasmodically reaches across her body for her shoulder. The motion coupled with the savage anger in her face captures an air of despondency and petulance identical to that I once observed in a very young, disturbed child, unable to cope with emotions larger than himself. The feeling one senses is far beyond rage, reaching back to something primal and terrifying. Marlene's erotic frenzy at the sound of the returning drums in the banquet scene is, to Sternberg's and her credit, again very direct, not concealed by veils or shadows. The sound track is effectively used to augment her panic, as the noise of the returning soldiers draws nearer.

When Amy looks for Cooper in the hospital and finally locates him in the café, the intertwined rhythms of image and sound perfectly complement each other and capture the fervid passions which are seething beneath the drama. After Cooper leaves the café, Sternberg shows Dietrich's face as she discovers from his table carving that he does, indeed, love her. You can almost see her change color in this moment of revelation, a shot which also reveals an actress of the highest magnitude.

Dietrich's pursuit of Cooper into the desert has been called by Andrew Sarris, "the most romantic gesture in Sternberg's visual vocabulary." It works dramatically because it comes at a moment of panic, one in a series of such moments, each of which has brought Amy closer to the brink. Sternberg says "the average human being lives behind an impenetrable veil and will disclose his deep emotions only in a crisis which robs him of control." Amy Jolly had hidden behind her veil for many years and many men, and her emergence, the sublimation of her fear and pride into her desire, is one of the most supremely romantic gestures in the art of our century. It is a measure of contemporary cynicism and decay that no artists today would dare what Sternberg and Dietrich accomplished in 1930.

"*Morocco, The Blue Angel* — never before has anyone leaped into such instant popularity as glorious, glamorous Marlene Dietrich, 'with the wisdom of the ages in her

DISHONORED (1931). As X-27

eyes.' " Thus read the copy for Paramount's *Photoplay* ad publicizing *Dishonored* in May, 1931. The great box office success of *Morocco* had finally prompted the U.S. release of *The Blue Angel* in January. By April and May *Photoplay* was already running articles like "Dietrich—How She Happened" and "The Perils of Marlene." The first of these quotes Marlene's Uncle Conrad on his pride over her international fame but also his concern "whether all that makes people really happy. Marlene is so terribly busy and she is away from her family so much . . ." The second piece examines the problems posed by the "Potsdam Peacherino's" overexposed limbs, warning Sternberg: "We can't see the genius for the legs."

Although it has many virtues, *Dishonored* is not up to the standard of the two films which preceded it. We are introduced to the "Potsdam Peacherino" by seeing those infamous legs standing in the rain. Before long she is in the clutches of Gustav von Seyffertitz, recreating a bit too archly the role of spy chieftain he had played for Garbo three years before in *The Mysterious Lady*. X-27—we never do find out her real name—is a cross between Lola-Lola and Amy Jolly, incorporating both the vulgar charm of the former and the melancholia of the latter. In fact, as Sarris points out, she is ultimately several characters self-consciously trying on "different roles for size and style." In Seyffertitz's office, which, for no apparent reason, resembles Baron Frankenstein's laboratory, Dietrich agrees to spy for her fellow Austrians: "I've had an inglorious life; it may become my good fortune to have a glorious death."

In a party sequence which presages the fiesta in *The Devil Is a Woman*, Dietrich (X-27) introduces herself to Warner Oland (a suspected enemy agent) by pricking his balloon and allowing him to blow his decidedly phallic noise maker at her. The relationship is clinched when Dietrich repeats her imitation of a clucking hen from the wedding sequence of *The Blue Angel*. Later that same night, X-27 having discovered evidence of his treachery, Oland obligingly blows his brains out after expressing regret over having the evening spoiled by their contradictory loyalties. Dietrich consoles him with the thought that "we might never have met."

The plot continues in this essentially silly vein, and the bulk of the film is concerned with Dietrich and Russian aviator and spy Victor McLaglen's efforts to outfox each other. Seyffertitz's warning that McLaglen is too clever to be trapped by a woman and the film's prologue stating that X-27's sex prevented her from being the greatest spy in history are borne out. Dietrich falls in love with McLaglen and must pay the penalty of death for allowing him to escape.

In addition to its plot liabilities, *Dishonored* is excessively talky and, for a Sternberg film, very cheap-looking. McLaglen and Dietrich are not a credible couple, and it is noteworthy that in his *Express to Hollywood* (Jarrolds, 1934), McLaglen mentions neither the film nor Marlene. (He does inform his fans, however, that he once met Greta Garbo at a party.) In one scene Dietrich tells McLaglen she would like to share her last few hours on earth with him. Her delivery is so unconvincing that Sternberg uncharacteristically cuts away from her in the middle of the speech. X-27 is supposed to be insincere at this point (it is her very falseness which excites McLaglen), but something seems to have gotten away from Sternberg at various moments in the film.

Dishonored, like *Blonde Venus* the following year, should be viewed as a failure only within the context of the five Sternberg-Dietrich masterpieces which surround them. It is visually the most stunning movie to be made in Hollywood in 1931, a year when most directors were still trying to absorb the lessons Sternberg had taught them with *Morocco*. The exquis-

DISHONORED (1931). With Victor McLaglen

DISHONORED (1931). X-27 faces the firing squad.

itely lit airport scene where Dietrich bids farewell to McLaglen and the firing squad sequence with its Academy Award-winning experiments in sound are more than slight compensation for the film's weaknesses.

Dietrich's performance becomes somewhat disjointed by the many guises she must assume, although in her Russian peasant masquerade one can see the rudiments of both her young Catherine (*The Scarlet Empress*) and her cockney tart (*Witness For the Prosecution*). She is hampered by not having any musical numbers, but rather the perversely passionate piano renditions Sternberg invokes to accentuate plot points. There is a glorious shot of Marlene and a cat with their heads together, both with identical

SHANGHAI EXPRESS (1932). With Clive Brook

expressions. (Earlier X-27 had been meowing in an attempt to seduce Lew Cody.) Her petulant gesture of throwing away an empty gun with which she hoped to shoot McLaglen recalls her drunk scene in *Morocco*, and she is magnificent dying in the uniform "I wore when I served my countrymen instead of my country," the dress of a woman of the streets.

Almost consciously, Sternberg seemed to be seeking something more outrageous than the ending of *Morocco*. With Barry Norton's anti-war speech being upstaged by Marlene's fixing her face and thighs for the firing squad, Sternberg is mocking the solemnity of such pacifist heroics as those expounded by Lew Ayres in *All Quiet on the*

Western Front. And with the ironic playing of the treacly "Anniversary Waltz" on the sound track as Dietrich's body lies bleeding in the snow following her "glorious death," Sternberg is asserting the primacy of X-27's cheap, ultimately free brand of love over the more conventional values of his audience. It was around this time that Mrs. Sternberg sued for divorce, and Dietrich was designated a "love pirate."

By February 1932 and the release of *Shanghai Express*, *Photoplay* was speculating on Dietrich's efforts to get out from under the "hypnotic spell" of her Svengali. It assured its readers that she was a loyal wife and mother who didn't love this "strange little man . . . a trifle mad—yet he comes darn close to being a genius." The screen Marlene, after all, is only "a figment of his imagination." The magazine also informed its following that Marlene had far more brains than Trilby ever had and could take care of herself.

Next to Lola-Lola, Shanghai Lily is probably Dietrich's most famous portrayal and contends for her finest performance. She is a notorious coaster, a kind of traveling whore. Five years earlier (before more than one man had changed her name to Shanghai Lily), she had had an affair with British officer Clive Brook which had ended unhappily because of his lack of trust in her. Now they are accidentally reunited on Sternberg's deliriously exotic train journeying from Peiping to Shanghai. Also on the train are a Chinese courtesan (Anna May Wong), an Eurasian merchant (Warner Oland), and several characters of various nationalities who provide comic relief and sit in moral judgment of Dietrich and Wong. It turns out that Oland is actually a revolutionary bandit whose forces intercept the train, holding the passengers hostage until Wong kills him.

If one chose to ignore the seething emotionalism of the Dietrich-Clive Brook relationship, there was enough that could pass for conventional melodrama and adventure here to calm the growing fears of some who felt this "genius" might be trying to contaminate their ninety minutes of diversion with Art. In retrospect, the needs of the plot and the requisite happy ending do impose certain limitations on the value of *Shanghai Express*, but it still represents one of the best compromises with commercial consideration ever to come from Hollywood. By the time of *The Scarlet Empress* and *The Devil Is a Woman*, Sternberg would no longer have any truck with compromise, and such arrogance would virtually wreck his career.

Generosity was not one of Sternberg's stronger qualities, understandable perhaps in light of the ingratitude and insensitivity to which he was generally subjected. Still, it might have been nice had his autobiography acknowledged men like Lee Garmes who photographed *Shanghai Express* (also *Morocco* and *Dishonored*) and Jules Furthman who helped write the film (along with *Morocco* and *Blonde Venus*). The sin is compounded by Sternberg's assertion that Harry Hervey's original treatment consisted of only one page. In fact, the Hervey material (available for study at the Museum of Modern Art) runs to twenty-two pages and contains a surprising number of elements which appear in the finished film.

Yet for all the contributions of

SHANGHAI EXPRESS (1932). With Anna May Wong

others, *Shanghai Express* remains a thoroughly personal statement on the part of Sternberg, one of his most personal, in fact. The film's thematic content and visual properties are pure Sternberg. With regard to the handling of actors, Clive Brook has recounted in several interviews going to the director with the assertion that all the participants were speaking in a dreary monotone. Sternberg replied: "Exactly, I want that. This is the Shanghai Express, and everyone must talk like a train." Such trivialities of plot as the machine-gunning of a regiment of solders are given typically short Sternbergian shrift. The director characteristically reserved both his passion and compassion for his lovers, whose obsessions were revolutionary enough for his taste.

It is not too far-fetched to view *Shanghai Express* as the mirror image of *Morocco*, the other major Sternberg/Furthman/Dietrich collaboration. Suppose Amy Jolly had not followed Gary Cooper into the desert! Suppose she had waited for him to come to her on her own terms! Clive Brook's very reticent military officer is a similar characterization to Cooper's Legionnaire Brown, although he is older and the possessor of a bit more perspective on his weltschmertz, more likely therefore to finally succumb to Dietrich's demand for love without conditions. Both films have the same inexorably obsessive flow of images to match the drama which is taking place. Both films afford Dietrich the opportunity to display her great gift for expressing vulnerability beneath a facade of strength.

Ambiguity is more of a factor in Dietrich's portrayal of Shanghai Lily than it was with Amy Jolly. Her motivation is never totally articulated, and she remains to the end an authentically mysterious lady. Yet, from her anxiety when she is fearful for Brook's life, a moment reminiscent of her engagement party frenzy in *Morocco*, Marlene's manner expresses far better than words her reawakened feelings for the man she loved five years before. When Brook presses her for an explanation as to why she consented to stay with Warner Oland before Anna May Wong does him in (Lily did it to save Brook from being blinded by the rebels), she refuses to bolster his sagging faith in her. He wants to know why she had prayed for him, a lovely shot showing only her hands immersed in shadow. She replies: "I would have done that for anybody."

There follows one of the most perfect expressions of Sternberg and Dietrich's collaborative skill. It is a beautiful closeup of Lily, now alone in her compartment, lit from below and surrounded by blackness. She has just risked all that she values in

SHANGHAI EXPRESS (1932). As Shanghai Lily

life in a show of will and gamble with fate, and although she retains her composure, there is the most delicate of tremors in her face, and a quivering in her hand as she puffs on the cigarette behind which Dietrich so often hides her fragility. For an instant we have encapsulized before us the terror of loneliness we all feel—and our competing pride, our need to deny dependence on resources not under our total command. Like Dietrich's recognition of Cooper's love through his table carving in *Morocco*, it is a subtle and sublime fragment of the highest cinematic art.

Dietrich's next film, *Blonde Venus* (1932), begins with the unlikely premise that Lola-Lola could settle down, be a good wife and mother, and content herself with domestic pleasures like giving little Dickie Moore a bath. Before the film returns full cycle to this improbability, it flirts with the notion that she'd much rather give one to Cary Grant.

The full impact of the Depression began to be felt by the final year of the Hoover administration, and Hollywood responded by showing its most glamorous ladies wallowing in squalor and degradation. Garbo in *Susan Lenox: Her Fall and Rise*, Bankhead in *Tarnished Lady*, Hopkins in *The Story of Temple Drake*—all were less fortunate than Dietrich who had a Sternberg to help her transcend and triumph over sordidness. The director's own youth had not been without its seedy Chaplinesque touches. These experiences he applied to *The Salvation Hunters*, in part a documentary on poverty, and by his own admission, he spent a night in the Bowery flophouse from which Dietrich suddenly emerges to resume her stardom after the requisite suffering.

The misery begins when Dietrich must return to the cabaret career of her youth to raise money so that husband Herbert Marshall can go off to Germany to be treated for a rare radiation disease, presumably one which causes him to give numerous tedious performances throughout the thirties. While Marshall is away, Marlene takes up with Cary Grant, who has everything Marshall doesn't, including enough money to pay for the cure. Grant is attracted to Dietrich by her incredible and nearly inaudible "Hot Voodoo" number, in which she transforms herself from a gorilla with a runny nose into the "Blonde Venus," part Afro, part Harpo. Although Grant is never less than gentlemanly and charming, he does succeed in seducing Dietrich away from her touching loyalty to her domestic responsibilities. Because, however, he has the ineffable qualities which Grant brings to any role even this early in his career, it is

SHANGHAI EXPRESS (1932). With Clive Brook

Marshall who becomes the cad for insisting on the fidelity that almost any man in 1932 considered to be a God-given right. Outraged by her faithlessness, he insists that she turn their child over to him. She flees with the boy, only to give him up later in a burst of maternal unselfishness. Through a number of plot convolutions, the film does arrive at a happy ending. If Marshall is a still-untrusting Clive Brook at the end, Grant is an ever-generous Adolphe Menjou. Since Dietrich is

allowed no outlet for genuine sexual passion in *Blonde Venus*, Dickie Moore is the film's Gary Cooper.

There is a hardness to Dietrich's performance here which doesn't return until *Manpower* a decade later, another excursion into contemporary American squalor. The demands of character and plot play away from her talent for conveying vulnerability, and only at the end when she has paid for her indiscretion is Marlene allowed a certain degree of elegance and glamour.

BLONDE VENUS (1932). As Helen Faraday

BLONDE VENUS (1932). With Herbert Marshall

When she loses the child to her husband after running away with the boy for nearly half the film, Sternberg does permit her a moment of maternal grief. At no point during the movie is she less than adequate. In fact, she and Sternberg are both so much better than the material that it must have been a great temptation to upstage the whole enterprise more than they do. It is only when Dietrich returns to being Dietrich, however, that one senses full creative involvement.

There are more than faint echoes of Lo Tinto's Moroccan café in the Parisian nightclub sequence in which Dietrich rises above her circumstances and returns to her natural state of stardom. In top hat and tuxedo, this time white, she manages to caress the cheek of a chorus girl. Grant rediscovers her and finds that she is now Amy Jolly, offstage as well as on. "I'm not in love with anybody, and I'm completely happy," she asserts. She is back in her dressing room, virtually the same one as in *The Blue Angel* and *Morocco*. There is the ever-present mirror, this time without Gary Cooper's farewell message but instead the inscription: "Down to Gehenna or up to the throne—He travels fastest who travels alone." Dietrich, like her mirror, has weltschmerz written all over her. She first declines Grant's offer to return to New York, putting back on her head the top hat which symbolizes her masculine independence, popping it to convey the same contempt for banal respectability the gesture expressed in *Morocco*. A newspaper story informs us, however, that she has changed her mind and now plans to marry Grant.

Throughout *Blonde Venus*, Sternberg's stylistic grace—his reasonably successful attempts to make the South exotic, some fine musical numbers, the picturesque magic of Bert Glennon's photography—prevent the film from going down the drain with the soap. His ending is in keeping with this skill, essentially avoiding the awful potential for sentimentality in the family reunion. When Dietrich, in elegant evening dress, washes Dickie Moore (she had bathed him in *hausfrau* attire earlier), she manages to be touchingly intimate without being maudlin. When it comes time for the final forgiving clinch between Marlene and Marshall, Sternberg wisely cuts away to Moore, who has dominated the sequence, and his tiny hand fingering his music box through the bars of his crib. It is credible to show Dietrich with that which is her obsession, but to show her at length with her husband would have been somehow obscene. Thus Sternberg and Dietrich, even in this little picture

BLONDE VENUS (1932). With Cary Grant

BLONDE VENUS (1932). With Hattie McDaniel

forced upon them by the demands of the marketplace, are able to confound their audience's expectations and subvert its values.

Is Dietrich through? In January 1933 this question was posed for the first, and certainly not the last, time. Sternberg had bailed Marlene out of *Blonde Venus*, finishing the picture even though he hated it, according to director Richard Wallace, the replacement Paramount had tried to impose on its star. Now Sternberg was talking about retirement, and Dietrich was speculating on a concert career in Europe. "I will never make pictures in America

with anyone but Mr. von Sternberg."

After strenuous effort, Sternberg and Paramount persuaded Dietrich to try working just once with another director. *Song of Songs* is sandwiched between two of Rouben Mamoulian's best films, *Love Me Tonight* with Maurice Chevalier and Jeanette MacDonald and *Queen Christina,* Garbo's finest performance before *Camille*. It is hard, therefore, within this context and the context of the Sternberg films not to view *Song of Songs* as a failure. The fact that Mamoulian seemed to consciously

SONG OF SONGS (1933). As Lily

SONG OF SONGS (1933). With Lionel Atwill

compete with Sternberg accentuates the film's inadequacies and presumptions.

The original source for *Song of Songs* was a novel by Hermann Sudermann, whose work had provided the inspiration for perhaps the greatest of silent films, F.W. Murnau's *Sunrise*. One can imagine that *Song of Songs* might have worked better as a silent also, but this is no excuse for the weakness of the script. Actually one of the writers, Samuel Hoffenstein, was later to contribute to the scintillating dialogue of Frank Borzage's post-Sternberg Dietrich film, *Desire*.

Brian Aherne tells an amusing story in his autobiography, *A Proper Job* (Houghton Mifflin, 1969) of being promised the lead in *Peter Ibbetson* (which finally went to Gary Cooper), if he would first get one other Hollywood film under his belt, *Song of Songs*. Being in awe of Dietrich, Aherne agreed to come to America without having read the script. When he finally did read it, he was overcome with despair and amazement that Marlene would consent to make such a film. When they finally met, she asked him, "Why have you come to do this silly picture . . . Are you crazy?" Her excuse was the requirements of her contract, and she was in awe of the stage actor and his freedom. Their friendship was cemented by their mutual plight and one of her Viennese cakes.

As could have been expected from this inauspicious beginning, shooting did not go smoothly. After some initial conflict, Mamoulian felt the need to assert his control over Aherne: "You will do what I say, and I will take full responsibility." In this atmosphere, Dietrich hid in her dressing room between takes, baking cakes, while, as Aherne puts it, "I went to mine to consider . . . how I could manage to bake Miss Dietrich." The upshot was that Paramount was so dissatisfied with *Song of Songs* that it bought up Aherne's contract to do *Peter Ibbetson*.

The plot revolves about the young, orphaned Dietrich's coming from the country to live with her aunt (Alison Skipworth) in Berlin. She is both innocent and religious, but before long she has agreed to model in the nude for Aherne, the neighborhood sculptor. Lionel Atwill plays a lascivious baron who buys the statue of Marlene and ultimately acquires the real thing, too. Rather like Sternberg's molding Dietrich, Atwill tries to make a proper baroness of his young, unsophisticated wife. She is unable to satisfy him, looking back to her pastoral[1] romance with the sculptor who had inexplicably rejected her. Finally Dietrich and Aherne are reunited, but not before Marlene has gone through the degradation of becoming a Sternbergian cabaret singer. (She performs the rather nice Hollander song, "Jonny," in English, even though Dietrich later was to insist in her concerts that no English words were ever written for it. She also claims this was the first song she ever recorded.) The life-sized nude statue is symbolically destroyed.

Tom Milne, in his study of Mamoulian (Indiana University Press, 1969), comments on "a basic uncertainty of conception in the film, which never quite makes up its mind whether it is opting for tender lyricism, stringent mockery of

SONG OF SONGS (1933). With Brian Aherne and Lionel Atwill

human fallibility, or simply melodramatic splendor." This sense that *Song of Songs* is a film of pieces which do not quite add up to a satisfactory whole is very strong. The opening expressionist scenes, an idyllic romp in the country with Aherne, and a spectacular sweeping crane shot in the cabaret sequence all are quite good in their own right, but their value is tempered by the self-consciousness of plot and characterization. For a film in which two men are madly in love with a woman, there is a peculiar lack of the obsessive tension always present in Sternberg. Aherne's performance is lightweight, and Atwill, who is superficially sympathetic and well-intentioned, is not allowed to be more than a gross caricature of Erich von Stroheim. Atwill's work in Sternberg's *The Devil Is a Woman*, a similar role two years later, is much more controlled and, therefore, more poignant.

Dietrich is good, although not as good as in the Sternberg films. Rather *Song of Songs* (somewhat like *Dishonored*) afforded her the opportunity to try on different roles such as the young innocent, and to further explore the depths of her coquetry. Such experimentation doubtless contributed to the subtle mastery she displayed in *The Scarlet Empress* and *The Devil Is a Woman*. There is also an overt erotic element introduced by Mamoulian. Although its most blatant manifestation is the nude statue and the suggestive things done to it, there are more delicate examples, such as the hint of a nipple outlined beneath Marlene's smock. Dietrich is always affecting, but the deficiencies of the script call for too-abrupt changes from naïveté to irony to corruption and back again to vulnerability. Furthermore, Mamoulian and cameraman Victor Milner, Lubitsch's favorite photographer in this period, did not take the care with Dietrich's face lavished on her by Sternberg. If for the eye shadows and wrinkles alone, it is not surprising that Trilby wanted to return to her Svengali after *Song of Songs*.

Sternberg has described *The Scarlet Empress* as "a relentless excursion into style." As such, it sacrificed some of the more ordinary virtues of even his own films for the sake of a grandiose form and a visual splendor verging on madness. *The Scarlet Empress* is the kind of work the cinema produces perhaps once in a decade—a film so far ahead of its time in ambition and scope that no one knows quite how to deal with it. Like Griffith's *Intolerance* (1916), Gance's *Napoleon* (1927), and Ophuls' *Lola Montes* (1955), it represents an artistic denouement, a literal explosion of creative energy and inspiration.

Sternberg's subject for his spectacle is Catherine the Great, "ill-famed Messalina of the North." She is, in fact, a combination of Napoleon and Lola Montes. In the opening sequence, Catherine is played by Dietrich's daughter Maria, then about nine years old. Although she is a Prussian princess, she is brought up on horror stories of Ivan the Terrible and Peter the Great. There is a splendid nightmare fantasy montage, Sternberg's anticipation of Hitchcock's *Marnie*.

Dietrich takes over the role of Catherine in young adulthood, just in time for her betrothal to the heir to the throne of Russia. In these sequences Marlene is a cross between the wide-eyed peasant girl of *Song of Songs* and a D.W. Griffith heroine, jumping up and down with excitement. The immediate cause of her enthusiasm is the arrival of the barbarically handsome John Lodge, emissary of the czarina, who is to escort her to Moscow. Even in her state of innocence and purity, Dietrich has an alert eye for men and their endowments.

The first half hour of *The Scarlet Empress* is concerned with the education of Catherine by her Polonius-like father (C. Aubrey Smith), her mother (Olive Tell), Lodge, and the czarina (Louise Dresser). Their intention is to domesticate her, to make her a proper wife to the emperor-to-be. The result is quite the opposite. Marlene Dietrich never needed to be taught how to be a woman, and as Catherine the Great, that part of her which could not be contained within the limitations of a single sex ultimately becomes politicized.

Although Sternberg graphically presents Catherine's journey to Moscow to convey the size of Russia, he somewhat anachronistically for 1934 uses long titles to suggest what the country is like—its op-

THE SCARLET EMPRESS (1934). As Catherine the Great

THE SCARLET EMPRESS (1934). Catherine in the palace

pressive history, etc. There are also
very complex montage sequences
throughout the film, very atypical of
Sternberg, but demonstrating the
fact that if he had wanted to make a
conventional historical film, he obviously could have. Essentially
these touches of brilliance are
thrown away by the director; they
are merely used to advance the plot
to a point more interesting to him.
The film's massive decor of death,
its uniquely brilliant black and
white photography, and Dietrich's
trifling with her men provide the
spectacle with which Sternberg is
truly concerned.

The palace Sternberg created for

THE SCARLET EMPRESS (1934). With Sam Jaffe

The Scarlet Empress is decorated with a grotesqueness matched only by its inhabitants. Sam Jaffe, the insane emperor-designate, roams the halls in command of his troop of live wooden soldiers. He is treated by Louise Dresser, his aunt, with the respect due a not-too-lovable dog, but since he will be emperor upon her death, she is concerned that he have a proper wife to insure the succession of her family line. She indulges Jaffe in his infantile behavior, even when he sticks a massively phallic drill through a religious painting to spy on her bedroom.

Characterization in *The Scarlet Empress* is thoroughly ironic (like almost everything else in the film) to the point of perversity. Dresser is pure Evansville, Indiana, testing to the limit the cliché that Americans and Russians are a very similar people in their primitive expansiveness. She archly plays the role of empress, performing the requisite ceremonies with typical Sternbergian knowingness and detachment, looking over her own shoulder and commenting on her behavior to anyone who cares or dares not to listen. Lodge, too, takes his ups and downs, his invitations to and ejections from her royal bedroom with reserve and dignity. There is no room for weltschmerz in the Kremlin. Sam Jaffe, to whom Dietrich is finally wed in an unconsummated marriage, is brilliant as a popeyed maniac whose values are essentially those of Sternberg's audience, wanting only a submissive wife who will bear him children.

Sternberg's control over *The Scarlet Empress* was as complete as could be achieved in Hollywood. He conducted the orchestra (the film has more music than usual) and when a violinist was needed for the wedding banquet, he composed the tune. The film's humor (when it is intended to be funny, it is as funny as any screwball comedy) is clearly his, from the cuckoo clock with the woman who exposes herself, to Dresser's grabbing a drumstick instead of her scepter. Although Bert Glennon, Sternberg's old compatriot from his silent days (*Underworld*, *The Last Command*), is given credit for the photography, one cannot help wondering what his contribution might have been, especially in light of Sternberg's solo effort on *The Devil Is a Woman*. Both of these films push black and white cinematography to its absolute limits.

The sequence in which Dietrich is married to Jaffe is as lovely as anything the cinema has ever offered. It is recommended to anyone who is in doubt about Sternberg's art. The director clutters his essentially horizontal rectangular frame with such vertical rectangles as double-barred crosses, religious

THE SCARLET EMPRESS (1934). With John Lodge

banners, and the hats of the priests. Yet despite all these religious trappings, the Jaffe/Dietrich/Lodge triangle predominates over the Christian spectacle. Jaffe leers at Dietrich and chomps salaciously on a holy wafer while Dietrich, gorgeous in extreme closeup behind her veil, tries unsuccessfully not to look at Lodge, the candle she is holding shaking and flickering from her hot breath. Dietrich's eyes and the invisible exhalation of her nostrils are more palpable and sacrosanct than the most ostentatious trappings of the Church. For just this once, the director stands in for both God and himself, and he declares Sternberg the victor.

With her marriage to Jaffe, Dietrich begins to dominate the film. She is still relatively naïve, still equating infidelity with wickedness. Lodge berates her for refusing his advances with: "Don't be absurd—those ideas are old-fashioned—this is the eighteenth century." She still believes in his goodness until the sequence in which Dresser has an unknowing Dietrich let Lodge into her bedroom. To do this Dietrich must descend a secret stairway at the bottom of which Lodge is waiting to be summoned to the royal bed. As Marlene passes through the doorway leading from the bedroom, the shadow of a statue of Satan is cast on

the secret passage, Sternberg's ironic comment on his audience's conception of evil. Dietrich is lit from above as she goes down the stairs to discover Lodge, and we have an unprecedented view of the wrinkles in her forehead. This visual suggestion of aging, the loss of youthful illusions, is followed immediately by Dietrich's giving herself to the captain of the guard, the father of the child who will become heir to the throne.

Following the birth of Dietrich's child, Sternberg perversely shows Dresser in bed behaving as though she were the mother. Then he cuts to Marlene with the infant, overlooked by a statue of the Madonna and her offspring. When Lodge comes to congratulate Catherine on the historic birth, a lady-in-waiting wryly comments on her certainty that "history was far from her mind at the time." By this point, it is fairly clear that history is equally far from Sternberg's mind.

Dietrich's transformation from innocence to irony to decadence parallels her too-rapid development in *Song of Songs*. Stylistic matters aside, we are compensated for any haste in *The Scarlet Empress* by the degree to which she savors each stage of growth. There is neither vacuity in her innocence nor guilt over its loss. Ultimately Catherine can reject the political support of the Church because she realizes she

THE DEVIL IS A WOMAN (1935). With Lionel Atwill

has weapons "far more powerful than any political machine." When she is warned that she doesn't know Russians, she responds suggestively that she is "taking lessons as fast as I can." When it is proposed that Jaffe's frustrated animosity might force her to take refuge in a convent, she replies, "Entirely too many men love my hair." In the outrageous scene in which she inspects the barracks, Dietrich looks Gavin Gordon up and down and then, focusing her eyes on his groin, informs him that she's heard a lot about him "from the ladies." For this he receives a medal for "bravery in action."

The culmination of all this scandalizing comes in the scene in which Jaffe strips Gordon, now Dietrich's consort, of his rank and sword for insubordination. Without cutting away, Sternberg's camera suddenly lowers its position. Whereas we previously saw Jaffe and Gordon from the waist up, we now also have their groins included in the frame. Thus Sternberg salaciously suggests that Gordon has not been deprived of the weaponry and qualifications for which Dietrich raised him up from the ranks in the first place.

Amidst Christian iconography, the clanging of bells, and the "Ride of the Valkyries" on the sound track, Dietrich becomes empress with all the vengeful fury of Griffith's Ku Klux Klan rescuing Lillian Gish from a fate worse than death. The last two reels are almost completely without dialogue, and Dietrich gives a large segment of one of her strongest performances without uttering a sound. After she rides victoriously into the palace and up the stairs, the penultimate shot of the film superimposes the triumphant Catherine over the image of Christ on the church ceiling. Finally she blots Him out, Sternberg's comment not just on Catherine the Great but undoubtedly also on this other provincial Prussian girl who had come to usurp his career, if not his life.

With *The Devil Is a Woman*, (1935) Sternberg and Dietrich finally rid themselves of each other. The film itself is something of a translation of their relationship into visual poetry and metaphor. Dietrich has steadfastly maintained that it is her favorite of the seven they made together. Sternberg in later life stated a preference for *Anatahan*, his last and most controversial film. One suspects that this choice is somewhat perverse, however, and it is no secret that a great deal of himself went into *The Devil Is a Woman*. Many observers have commented on the obvious physical similarity between the director and his two male protagonists, Lionel Atwill and Cesar Romero.

This film is not as warm as

THE DEVIL IS A WOMAN (1935). With Cesar Romero

Morocco or as accessible as *The Blue Angel*. It is perhaps the most perfect film ever made in some ways, yet its very perfection conveys a coldness, a diamond-like hardness. The romanticism of *Morocco* has become transformed into cynical introspectiveness and fatalism. If Sternberg is any closer to understanding Dietrich, he is unwilling to solve the puzzle for the audience. *The Devil Is a Woman* remains the most beautifully realized enigma in the history of the cinema. If, as Hemingway said, Dietrich "knows more about love than anyone," let us not forget that she is always insisting that Sternberg taught her everything she knows.

The film is set at the beginning of the century, at carnival time in southern Spain. The superb Edward Everett Horton as the officious governor is one of the few overtly humorous characters in any Sternberg movie. Perhaps the director felt a need to lighten the somberness of the main story. It was largely Sternberg's treatment of Horton and the *Guardia Civil* under his command that caused Paramount to withdraw the film from distribution under pressure from the Spanish government. Only through fortuitous circumstances was the film preserved from total destruction.

The complex imagery of the carnival had been rehearsed by Stern-berg in *Underworld* and *Dishonored*, and Dietrich's first meeting with Romero recalls her liaison with Warner Oland in the latter film. Concha Perez has no other excuse for living, except as an embodiment of eroticism. She is the least intelligent and the most guileful of the roles Sternberg created for Dietrich. One cannot imagine that she would ever want to be an empress or could ever cope with domestic responsibilities. She exists solely to lure men after her, allow them to catch up, and then run away again. If Shanghai Lily was a whore with a heart of gold, Concha, "the toast of Spain," is pure whore, with no redeeming organs whatsoever. Her only saving grace is that she never conceals her motivation, at least until the end of the film.

The Devil Is a Woman (Sternberg had intended to call it *Capriccio Espagnol*) takes the form of the older Atwill warning the younger Romero of Concha by telling in flashback the many instances in which she had humiliated him. "She's the most dangerous woman you'll ever meet," he informs Romero. Atwill is something like Adolphe Menjou, but Sternberg allows him no charm or humor. He is as Menjou might have been after Amy Jolly had gone through several dozen legionnaires and returned to his protection after each, or as

THE DEVIL IS A WOMAN (1935). With Don Alvarado

Sternberg perhaps was after seven films with Dietrich, five of which were more or less forced upon him.

During the course of his narration, Atwill is playing with a male puppet on a stick, forcing it to assume positions evocative of an orgasm. The implication is clearly that Concha has played with him in the same manner, manipulating him and depriving him of his freedom to act. One wonders if Sternberg is not also commenting on the nature of his actors, since he goes to some length in his book and elsewhere to define them as mere marionettes, totally dependent on him for control and inspiration. Of Dietrich, for example, he writes in *Fun in a Chinese Laundry*: "No puppet in the history of the world has been submitted to as much manipulation as a leading lady of mine who, in seven films, not only had hinges and voice under a control other than her own but the expression of her eyes and the nature of her thoughts." If, indeed, *The Devil Is a Woman* gives something of an accurate picture of the Sternberg-Dietrich off-screen relationship, then one can more fully appreciate the rewards for Sternberg of being on the set where he could keep a firm hold on the strings.

Dietrich's song, "I'm Romantic —Three Sweethearts Have I," fits the mocking tone of the film. Atwill is always aware of his foolishness,

obsessed with his very obsessiveness. He knows he can never trust Concha, but he is always shattered when this is borne out. As he tells her, "Life without you means nothing to me." It is the harsh other side of Menjou's, "You see I love her. I'd do anything to make her happy." Life with Concha on her terms is also meaningless and tormenting, but Atwill is unable or unwilling to free himself from her spell. He is even made to feel guilty for his continued existence. After one betrayal Concha comes to him in the morning with the reprimand: "If you had loved me enough, you would have killed yourself last night."

One of the great virtues of *The Devil Is a Woman* and one of the problems it has with audiences is its compactness. There are no melodramatic subplots as there were in *Shanghai Express* to cushion the blow or sugarcoat the pill. The film is as raw as the emotions it portrays, as raw as the wounds Concha blithely inflicts.

Perhaps the greatest irony of the film is that all the while Atwill is telling Romero how Dietrich has ruined his career and made a nightmare of his life, he is planning to resume his liaison with her. One is never sure where his concern for Romero leaves off and his feeling of rivalry begins. Ultimately this conflict results in Concha's greatest

With Ernest Hemingway in the late thirties

triumph: a duel over her between the two friends, in which Atwill is seriously wounded.

How can one interpret Dietrich's change of heart and mind at the end of *The Devil Is a Woman?* She visits Atwill in the hospital where he rejects her for the first time. This is enough in itself to excite and fascinate her. There is a long closeup of Dietrich's face behind a veil, musing over this behavior which she has never had to confront before. Later when we see her having wine with Romero while awaiting the train that will take them to Paris, she is subdued and serious, the antithesis of the Concha we have previously experienced. Whether Sternberg is suggesting that she has matured or reformed is never made explicit. As Romero's train leaves, Dietrich, her face partially veiled in smoke, begs forgiveness: "I'm going back to Pasqual. Try and forget me, Antonio." She tells the customs officials: "I've changed my mind." Ostensibly, she has decided to return to Atwill in the hospital.

Perhaps Sternberg is suggesting that it is inconceivable in the final analysis that Dietrich could reject his stand-in or himself. One should remember that during the five years of their professional relationship, it was always Sternberg who insisted that they had worked together long enough. On the other hand, all that we know of Concha until the end of the film was conveyed through the eyes and the mouths of the men. Perhaps these were all lies, and now we are seeing her for the first time as she really is. And since we never see Dietrich reunited with Atwill, we don't even know whether she was telling Romero the truth.

Such speculation suggests the obvious point that none of us ever really does fully understand what goes on inside the head of another. After seven films or seven lifetimes together, there still is no satisfactory way to bridge the gap, even with a paradoxical and mystical quip like "Miss Dietrich is me—I am Miss Dietrich." Whatever *The Devil Is a Woman* means, it means an end. Dietrich was to go on to make two dozen more films and to create one of the century's most enduring myths. Still, she was known upon occasion to cry out in frustration for Jo—the man she wanted to please most.

Sternberg's career took a fast and almost unredeemed nosedive. Nearly all of his best films are those he made with Dietrich, and no amount of verbal description or analysis can do them justice. As Peter Bogdanovich has said: " . . . more than any other director's work Sternberg's is what it appears to be. His images are complex and evocative, and the visual poetry of his films is either understood and appreciated as greatness, or not understood and dismissed as fancy, indulgent decoration."* I cast my lot for the former, and I would not doubt that the woman who embodied the most sublime figments of his imagination would feel the same.

*Peter Bogdanovich, "Encounters with Josef von Sternberg," *Movie*, #13, p.24.

In 1935 Ernst Lubitsch became production head of Paramount Pictures. Among his first tasks was to find a project for the newly liberated Dietrich. From a German film called *Die Schönen Tage Von Aranjuez* (The Beautiful Days of Aranjuez) the producer had three scenarists fashion the witty script which ultimately became *Desire*. (The original had starred Brigitte Helm, who reportedly had been one of those considered by Sternberg for Lola-Lola.) Whatever its antecedents may have been, however, *Desire* now impresses strongly as a sweetly romantic expression of the personality of its director, Frank Borzage.

Although Borzage's directorial career dated back to 1915, he had been little more than a journeyman until his great success at the very end of the silent era with *Seventh Heaven* (1927) and *Street Angel* (1928). These tender love stories, both starring Janet Gaynor and Charles Farrell, are among those Hollywood films which best illustrate the stage of near-perfection the studio-produced silents had reached just as talkies were bullying their way in. The cinema had never seen purer expressions of sincere romanticism, and *Desire* (like several other of Borzage's thirties films from *A Man's Castle* to *Three Comrades*) largely recaptures these feelings. When Dietrich tells John Halliday, "Love gives you strength and courage—something to fight for," she does it with the conviction that only a Borzage character can bring to such a line. And when she tells Gary Cooper, "We had a gorgeous week together—seven heavenly days—seven dreams," she is explicitly evoking both the director's earlier masterpiece and a whole Borzagian universe where time and reality mean nothing to two people in love.

In 1936 America was still in the depths of the Depression, and one wonders how well Gary Cooper's Bronson Eight song praising "a car for the masses" went over with audiences. Furthermore, *Desire's* concerns are so far removed from anything resembling social content (there is never an inkling that Spain, where most of the film takes place, will soon be the scene of a bloody civil war), that one can begin to understand how this and the films which followed it eventually alienated Dietrich from the public. Even when Marlene must pay for her crime at the end, her jail sentence is only a second of screen time. At one point in the film she asserts her belief in fairy tales, and that is essen-

DESIRE (1936). With Gary Cooper

DESIRE (1936). With Gary Cooper and John Halliday

tially what *Desire* is. Hans Dreier's sets and Travis Banton's costumes are lavish; Marlene's lighting and makeup are never less than ethereal. No matter how many convolutions there are to the plot, there is a blissfully happy ending. It is no accident that Hollander and Robin's lovely song for her in this film is called "Awake in a Dream."

The opening sequences of *Desire* clearly reflect the film's Lubitsch-like planning. We are returned four years later to the Paris of Lubitsch's great *Trouble in Paradise*, a Paris of suave jewel thieves and picturesque René Clair rooftops under which we find automotive engineer Cooper, about to set out on his vacation in Spain. We are introduced to him

DESIRE (1936). With John Halliday

and his boss, Bill Frawley, as they are engaged in a vociferous silent argument. The camera moves in and watches them from outside their window so that we hear nothing of what is said, a Lubitsch touch borrowed from the earliest days of sound. Before long Marlene has appeared and convinced both a nerve specialist (Alan Mowbray) and a jeweler (Ernest Cossart) that she is married to the other, while she has made off with a 200,000-franc string of pearls. There is an hysterically funny scene of recognition between Dietrich's two "husbands," revolving around her story to Mowbray about Cossart's inclination toward wearing nightgowns and presenting bills

DESIRE (1936). With Gary Cooper

to strangers. With the dissolve to Marlene's heading for Spain in her roadster, however, Lubitsch is left behind, and Spain itself has changed quite a bit from *The Devil Is a Woman*.

Cooper and Dietrich, now a "countess," cross paths. Although she manages to humiliate him, he accidentally and unknowingly winds up with the pearls. When Cooper catches up with her on the Riviera, Marlene has joined her accomplice, John Halliday. Together the two thieves try to get back the pearls while Cooper, by now infatuated, tries to get Dietrich. In spite of Halliday's warnings not to mix love with business, Marlene begins to waver. Her growing affection for Cooper plus a desire to reform cause her to confess to him. This results in an off-screen spanking and his assistance in returning the pearls to their owner. Halliday and Zeffie Tilbury, the crone who is used to represent what Marlene might have become if she remained a crook, are foiled. Following a stint in jail, Dietrich joins Cooper in Detroit where, one assumes, they live happily ever after.

Obviously, the great virtues of *Desire*, like Dietrich's Sternberg films, do not lie in its plot. And although Borzage loses little of the visual allure his predecessor captured in the actress, *Desire* looks like a Poverty Row production next to *The Devil Is a Woman*. Yet, there is something ineffably charming about the interaction between Cooper and Dietrich. Six years earlier, in *Morocco*, Cooper's stiffness as an actor in early talkies had been made into a virtue by Sternberg, since Legionnaire Brown's characterization required reserve and aloofness. Tom Bradley is the exact opposite, a chivalrously naïve and normal American, the perfect counterpart of Dietrich's Continentally corrupt cynic. Cooper had by now acquired that quality of freedom as an actor/personality which was to mark his most memorable performances, beginning with his very next film, *Mr. Deeds Goes to Town*.

Dietrich makes fools of all the men in the first half of the film. As Cooper is winning her over with his gallantry and innocence, however, we begin to see things which Sternberg never allowed. There are extended romantic sequences done largely with the two stars alone in semi-closeup. Many of the takes are long and apparently somewhat improvised, free from the manipulation of the puppeteer. After an exquisite scene on a moonlit balcony which cements their relationship, the realization begins to dawn for anyone who might have doubted it that Dietrich can act. There is a new vigorous air of playfulness in her performance, and as her character liberates herself from her life of

I LOVED A SOLDIER (uncompleted, 1936).

crime, Marlene frees herself of Sternberg's strings.

Dietrich's next film was to have been *I Loved a Soldier*, a remake of the silent Pola Negri vehicle *Hotel Imperial*. She was to play opposite Charles Boyer, under Henry Hathaway's direction. Shooting was abandoned after a month of conflict between Paramount and Marlene, and the film was ultimately made three years later with Isa Miranda.

It was around this time also that Dietrich inaugurated Cecil B. DeMille's Lux Radio Theater, appearing opposite Clark Gable in "The Legionnaire and the Lady."

David O. Selznick had been planning a remake of Rex Ingram's silent film, *The Garden of Allah*, for years. The project had been offered to Greta Garbo, who had rejected it as antiquated. Merle Oberon had also been considered. The plot concerned a sheltered and very religious European woman who tries to find the meaning of life following the death of her father by journeying to the desert. She meets, falls in love with, and marries a monk who has run away from a Trappist monastery. He is the sole possessor of the recipe for the liqueur on which the monastery's economy is

With Clark Gable, on a set in the mid-thirties

based. Finally his past catches up with him, and he returns to his vows, forsaking the outside world. The original version, starring Alice Terry and Ivan Petrovich, had actually been photographed in Algeria by Lee Garmes, whose camera mastery was later to contribute so much to the exoticism of *Morocco*, *Dishonored*, and *Shanghai Express*. Selznick planned to shoot his version in Arizona and use it to test his ideas about color (three-color Technicolor had just been perfected) which bore fruit three years later in *Gone With the Wind*.

Selznick chose as his director Richard Boleslawski, a Polish émigré who had directed films in Russia and acted with the Moscow Art Theatre. Through "Boley's" efforts and those of dialogue director Joshua Logan (and $200,000), Dietrich was persuaded to do the film, even though she is said to have considered it "twash." Charles Boyer, after fifteen years of screen acting, was now on the brink of becoming a major star. The distinguished cast was rounded out by Basil Rathbone, Joseph Schildkraut, C. Aubrey Smith, John Carradine, and Tilly Losch, performing a forerunner of the erotic dance she was to do in Selznick's *Duel in the Sun* a decade later.

Apparently both Boyer and Dietrich balked repeatedly at the script, and Selznick had no patience whatsoever with Marlene's Sternberg-taught concern with camera angles, lighting, and other production values. His insensitivity resulted in tactless memos containing foolish assertions such as the superiority of all his previous films over all of Dietrich's. Selznick would have no truck with the actors' "ridiculous assumption that they know anything about script." The dialogue of which he was so protective was, in the words of one critic, "obviously written by Alf Landon."

What is good about *The Garden of Allah*, that is, what makes it bearable, are precisely those areas over which Dietrich lavished such concern. Seen recently at Radio City Music Hall in a vintage 35mm color print, the film is visually stunning. Hal Rosson, the photographic adviser with whom Marlene was accused of conspiring, had worked with Sternberg on his great silent *Docks of New York* and two other now-lost films. He was to continue on to do the burning of Atlanta for Selznick and such great color musicals as *The Wizard of Oz* and *Singin' in the Rain*. *The Garden of Allah* was certainly an important opportunity for training and experimentation (Rosson and cameraman W. Howard Greene received a special Academy Award), and one can only speculate on what Marlene and this other disciple of Sternberg might have taught each other.

THE GARDEN OF ALLAH (1936). As Domini

THE GARDEN OF ALLAH (1936). With Charles Boyer

Both the ersatz exoticism and phony romanticism of the film bespeak a failed attempt to recapture the mystique of *Morocco*. But, as with *Song of Songs*, there is no obsessive tension in the acting and mise-en-scène to justify lines like "No one is bad who loves," or "No one but God and I know what is in my heart." Boleslawski, who had done a tolerably good film with Garbo (*The Painted Veil*), lingers too long over such claptrap, accentuating its absurdity. As Dietrich and Boyer's caravan wanders tediously through the desert, long, schmaltzy transitional titles appear on the screen which, combined with Max Steiner's overemphatic score, destroy what little credibility is left to the plot. Within this context, even the visuals become excessive as, for example, when Dietrich is lit like a madonna during

77

THE GARDEN OF ALLAH (1936). With Basil Rathbone and Joseph Schildkraut

the marriage ceremony or when she is surrounded by an orange halo as C. Aubrey Smith tells her, "I think you are made of fire." By the time of Boyer's exposure and the final renunciation scene, the logical flaws of the plot have become far too evident, and Boyer's moving breakdown into tears loses the effect his fine performance deserves.

Dietrich herself is not bad, although she is curiously stiff by comparison with *Desire* and with Garbo's spontaneity in *The Painted Veil*. Boleslawski, whose promising career was cut short by death the following year, allowed at least one ghastly shot to get past his editors. Dietrich's expression of horror that a monk could betray his vows is so overdone that it represents one of the worst moments in any of her films. Marlene is simply not at her best in conveying the banal kind of purity called for in the character of Domini. She gets away with naïveté in the early sections of *Song of Songs* and *The Scarlet Empress*, but virtue is not totally within the range of her virtuosity. Ultimately, when she is forced to cry real tears, Dietrich's lack of conviction is symptomatic of the humorless self-consciousness of the film. In the case of *The Garden of Allah*, one lovely pastel image of Marlene in a blue negligee on a balcony is worth several thousand purple words of David O. Selznick's pretentiously scripted baloney.

By 1937 Alexander Korda was the most powerful man in the British cinema. Largely through his lavish productions starring Charles Laughton, this Hungarian refugee had attained sufficient standing to make him the only British film-maker able to even fantasize competing with Hollywood. The importation of Marlene Dietrich to appear in his most expensive film, *Knight Without Armour*, was an unprecedented coup. Ironically, this came on the heels of the *I, Claudius* fiasco, the unfinished film for which Sternberg had been brought over to direct Laughton, whom Korda no longer could manage.

Knight was based on James Hilton's *Without Armour*. (Hilton's *Lost Horizon* was filmed by Frank Capra in Hollywood the same year.) It is the story of an English reporter-turned-spy caught up in the Russian Revolution. He meets a discounted countess amidst the maelstrom. They fall in love in the process of rescuing each other from the contending sides—she from Red captivity, and he from White. Finally they escape through the unlikely assistance of a sensitive young Bolshevik romantic and the Red Cross. Some elements of the plot bear curious similarities to *Dr. Zhivago*.

Dietrich had already appeared briefly in two Korda silent films made in Germany in 1926. The first of these, *A Modern Du Barry*, was from a story by Lajos Biro who was co-scenarist for *Knight Without Armour*. There was, therefore, a feeling of reunion about the production. When Korda threatened to replace Robert Donat (star of *The 39 Steps* and *The Ghost Goes West*) as the male lead because of a debilitating siege of asthma, Marlene intervened in his behalf. According to Korda's biographer, Paul Tabori, she dubbed Donat "Our Knight Without Asthma" upon his return from sickbed four weeks later. The several beautifully achieved and mellow moments between the two actors vindicate Dietrich's insistence on not replacing her co-star.

Jacques Feyder, a Hollywood career behind him and famous at the time for his *Carnival in Flanders,* directed the film competently

THE GARDEN OF ALLAH (1936). With Charles Boyer

KNIGHT WITHOUT ARMOUR (1937). With Robert Donat

KNIGHT WITHOUT ARMOUR (1937). With Austin Trevor (at her left)

if impersonally. Its novelistic structure is compensated for by strong visuals, somewhat derivative of Soviet films of the Revolution which had reached the West. For a film shot in England, it does have a surprisingly strong feel for the Russian reality, marred somewhat by the overly British manner of some of the supporting actors. Ultimately the Revolution becomes little more than a backdrop for a love affair.

There is an unparalleled amount of quasi-nudity in Feyder's treatment of Dietrich. A lovely sequence in which the countess awakens to find her servants have run away, the revolution having transpired over night, is capped with glorious shots of Marlene, long hair and white robe flowing in the wind, swooping across her enormous deserted estate in panic. As she runs toward the camera, the swaying of her breasts makes it evident that she is braless, and all the more beautiful for it. Later she bathes seductively in a tub, following her escape from the Reds, a sequence which ran into censorship problems in America. There is also a very distant shot of total nudity as Marlene (or a double?) swims in the woods like Hedy Lamarr in *Ecstasy.* Whether this form of exposure was called for or not, it did provide Dietrich with a sexuality quite unlike the tantalizing variety of the Sternberg films. Even Mamoulian, with the nude

statue and its perverse implications in *Song of Songs,* was not nearly so explicit. Of course, the effect of *Knight Without Armour* is the demystification of Marlene, soon to be fully realized in *Destry Rides Again.*

As usual, in the films preceding *Destry,* events, even revolutions, do not mar Marlene's beauty or the perfection of her coiffure. Despite this recurring annoyance, Feyder achieves some very pleasing lighting effects and directorial touches. While Donat and Dietrich wait anxiously to escape on a train from a deserted station, he recites Browning, and she responds with a pessimistic Russian poem. It is a poignant moment intended to contrast Donat's English optimism with her Russian hopelessness. Marlene is lit from below, and the shot reminds one of the exquisite image of Lily in *Shanghai Express* as she has just risked all to win her man on her terms; and Sternberg's camera contemplates the serene terror of her expression. Shortly thereafter, the countess must shoot a man to save Donat, and then they must part just as she is beginning to realize that she loves him. Marlene's face assumes the same posture of resoluteness it had as she prepared to follow her man into the desert at the climax of *Morocco,* and she makes the same graceful motion with her arm, slinging her possessions, in this case her cape, over her shoul-

KNIGHT WITHOUT ARMOUR (1937). With Herbert Lomas

der. Later, to facilitate their escape, Dietrich disguises herself as a cossack, a return to the role reversal of the Sternberg films. Cigarette in mouth and striding boldly through the soldiers' camp, she proves again that when the need or mood arose, she could be as much of a man as any male.

Angel (1937) is one of Dietrich's more underrated films and performances. It is very atypical Ernst Lubitsch, and also the culmination of that tendency in Marlene's post-Sternberg period to play roles more suited to Greta Garbo. Angel is a woman largely divested of Dietrich's great gifts for irony and perverse humor, a person of paradox who is enigmatic yet ultimately conventional. She dabbles in infidelity twice and both times she inexplicably rejects her potential lover for the husband with whom she has not achieved happiness. Herbert Marshall as her diplomat husband and Melvyn Douglas as her debonair "lover" are both too uninteresting to be worthy of her, and neither relationship strikes many sparks. Still, *Angel* is a successful film. Why?

To begin with, the film has a stylistic elegance, a quality for which Lubitsch is often not given enough credit. It was photographed by Charles Lang who shot not only *Desire*, but such other ultra-romantic Paramount movies of the era as *A Farewell to Arms* and *Peter Ibbetson*. When Marlene first comes to Laura Hope Crews' refined Parisian salon and flesh market, the camera remains discreetly outside and gracefully tracks from window to window as Ms. Crews moves through the various rooms of her establishment. (A whorehouse, no matter how tastefully furnished or administered, is perhaps best surveyed from the outside first.) As the film moves on to a gracious restaurant, an atmospheric park in the Parisian night, Ascot, and the like, *Angel* retains its subdued luster, the visual equivalent of the life style and mores it explores.

For Ernst Lubitsch, the film marked a return to directing after three years of producing. Although the film is hardly without his comic touch, most of the humor is centered in the peripheral characters of the servants, thus leaving the central drama very serious. (There is, for example, a splendid scene in which the servants in the kitchen read vast significance into the eating habits of their betters as the dinner plates are returned one by one from the dining room.) The clever repartee between Dietrich and Douglas when they first meet is very much like that in a similar scene in Lubitsch's *Ninotchka* (between Garbo and Douglas) which was made two years later. Douglas proceeds to show Marlene Paris, just as

85

KNIGHT WITHOUT ARMOUR (1937). As Alexandra

ANGEL (1937). With Herbert Marshall

he was to do for Garbo in the later film.

Herbert Marshall, after his graceful performance in Lubitsch's *Trouble in Paradise* (1932), had become the screen's most neglectful and cheated-upon husband. His profession had almost cost him Garbo in *The Painted Veil*, and he had almost lost Dietrich to Cary Grant in *Blonde Venus*. Of course, as one of the cinema's less scintillating stars, it seldom became credible how he won such women in the first place. In the case of *Angel*, Lubitsch makes things interesting (and, at the same time, dull) by making the alternative, Douglas, a kind of mirror image of the husband. The director frequently photographs them together in contemplative two-shots to emphasize their bland

ANGEL (1937). With Edward Everett Horton

sameness and contrast their dreariness with the glamorous image of Dietrich he projects. As it later turns out, the two men shared the same woman once before, during the war in France (Paulette called them Poochy and Schnooky), and the film is filled with an improbable stagelike symmetry of this order.

The camera placement and banter of Marlene's reunion scenes with Marshall echo those of her "infidelity" scenes with Douglas, again accentuating the banality of the choices open to her. Both men call her Angel, and both are so hopelessly sure of themselves that they are maddeningly sure of her, too. When Douglas and Marshall finally meet they strike up an immediate warm friendship—the logical outcome of two men so self-involved that they cannot help but respond favorably to their virtual twin. By today's liberated standards, *Angel* is a blatantly male-chauvinist film. One's acceptance of *Angel* as transcending its outrageous content depends on one's responsiveness to Lubitsch's masterful directorial style and to Dietrich's subtle performance.

The measure of a great actor or actress often is best taken in off-moments, when the camera almost isn't even looking. No one, save perhaps Chaplin, can convey so much with her back turned or merely with her hands as Dietrich. Yet the fragile elements which make Angel one of her most perceptive creations were precisely the delicacies too rich for thirties' audiences, the nuances which were to make her box-office poison. It matters little that *Angel* was a flop in the marketplace, except that something special about Dietrich was lost in subsequent films. It matters even less that Angel, in Lubitsch's con-

ANGEL (1937). With Ernest Cossart and Herbert Marshall

ANGEL (1937). With Melvyn Douglas

ception, is doomed to a life of sophisticated boredom. If marriage is not inevitably the death of romance, at least, one can hardly conceive of a creature of Dietrich's magnitude fitting comfortably within the confines of any relationship. And, as Angel says, "if the beginning is so beautiful, I wonder if the end matters."

At one moment in the film, Marshall suggests that Douglas get Dietrich's advice on the mysterious woman he met in Paris: "It's always good to get a woman's point of view." *Angel* is very much a movie about point of view. It is not unfair to assume that to a significant extent the two men represent Lubitsch perhaps more than he would have liked to admit. Despite all of his gallantry displayed through an illustrious career, Lubitsch's morality always remained very Old World, very Jewish, very male. The best he can offer Angel here is Marlene's line: "It's a privilege of a woman not to make sense. Men who expect a woman to be logical are likely to be failures in love." Lubitsch condescends to allow Marshall to forgive Dietrich's supposed infidelity, the attitude of a moralistic yet civilized man who looks at a woman and can only allow himself to see a lady.

In the end Marlene opts to accept his forgiveness and return to the tedium of their marriage with little reason to believe that there will be an improvement. In similar moments of enigmatic decision at the emotional climax of *Morocco* and *The Devil Is a Woman*, Sternberg lingers long and painstakingly on Dietrich's face, as if seeking to penetrate to her soul and join her there. In *Angel* we never see Marlene's face as she decides or afterward. One could speculate that Lubitsch might have taken this course through some feeling of the actress' limitations. Rather, I would suggest that the limitations were his own. Lubitsch could not find within himself sufficient identification with Angel's predicament. He could not be Angel and, therefore, could not breathe into Marlene the necessary feeling. We have here an excellent example of one of the major factors which, stylistics aside, separates a very good artist like Lubitsch from a great one like Sternberg—simply put, the androgyny of Sternberg's soul.

In July 1938 *Look* ran a picture spread entitled "Marlene Dietrich's Troubles." Not being the last word in tact, the article reported that Paramount had told Marlene "never to darken its cameras again." It ranked her current box-office draw on a par with Slim Summerville. There were reports on her love affairs, her wrinkles, and a vague plan to form a British production company to be headed by a fellow named Josef von Sternberg. 1938 was also the year of the famous motion picture exhibitors' ad defining Joan Crawford, Katharine Hepburn, and Dietrich as box-office poison.

Joe Pasternak had met Marlene in Berlin during the shooting of *The Blue Angel*, and in the process of trying to cast his Universal production of *Destry Rides Again* in 1939, it occurred to him that there might be a role for her. His account in his autobiography *Easy the Hard Way* (Putnam, 1956) recalls locating Dietrich on the Riviera in retirement and being rebuffed in suggesting the ridiculous idea of having her return to the screen in a remake of a Tom Mix western. She apparently didn't begin to believe in the project until the moment Pasternak taught her to roll her own cigarettes with one hand.

Marlene was cast opposite James Stewart, on the brink of superstardom (this was also the year of *Mr. Smith Goes to Washington*), and Charles Winninger, Mischa Auer, and Billy Gilbert were to provide comic relief. The plot deals with the rather passive efforts of deputy sheriff Stewart to clean up the town of Bottleneck which was being run into the ground by Brian Donlevy. Dietrich plays Frenchy, the singer in Donlevy's Last Chance Saloon, who obviously also provides other services for her boss. *Destry* was a novel idea, far more so than we can appreciate in an era where there are more spoofs made than actual westerns. (As this is being written, *Blazing Saddles* is amusing audiences with Madeline Kahn's parody of Dietrich, Lili von Shtupp.) The most extraordinary thing about *Destry*, though, was the new Dietrich.

The key to Frenchy's character, like that of Lola-Lola, is vulgarity. Our introduction to her comes in a scene where she is seated on the bar singing "Little Joe." (Pasternak wisely reunited Marlene with composer Friedrich Hollander.) Auer slaps her on the back, and she throws a drink in his face. She plunks her gambling winnings into her bosom. (The line, "There's gold

DESTRY RIDES AGAIN (1939). As Frenchy

in them thar hills," was cut.) Dietrich's humiliation is made complete by her extended fight with Una Merkel. The two women scratch and claw (Director George Marshall says Dietrich kept urging Merkel: "Push my face in the dirt . . . sit on me!"), and ultimately Frenchy gets a bucket of slop water poured over her. She specifically tells Stewart: "Don't call me a lady!" It was the denial of her previous image through such de-glamorizing that kept Dietrich's career alive, but there are moments in *Destry*

when one wonders if she isn't paying too high a price.

Stewart, who was to play a similar character to Destry in John Ford's great *The Man Who Shot Liberty Valance* a quarter century later, is excellent. At one point, Dietrich's black maid says quite presciently: "That's the peculiarest-acting man I ever did see—but he's got personality." Stewart works well with Dietrich. Her reformation to the extreme of giving up her life for him is not quite credible, but this is more a fault of Marshall's pedestrian direc-

DESTRY RIDES AGAIN (1939). With Brian Donlevy and James Stewart

DESTRY RIDES AGAIN (1939). With James Stewart

tion than of the two leads. *Destry*, like *Seven Sinners* and *Flame of New Orleans* to follow, is a fragile blending of genres. It is never consistently funny enough to be totally acceptable as a comedy, and only intermittently sincere enough to be engaging as a drama. Tay Garnett was to transcend these problems in *Seven Sinners* through his visual flair, his total immersion in the raucous potential of his material, and a genuine feel for the real emotions of people. Marshall was

DESTRY RIDES AGAIN (1939). With Una Merkel

merely a technician, and in spite of its many virtues, *Destry Rides Again* suffers from a flatness of imagination and élan.

The film does provide an interesting chapter in the relationship between Dietrich and her adopted homeland. Except for the exotic milieu of *Blonde Venus*, this was Marlene's first film with an American locale. Although native audiences were sure to view the new Dietrich as more humanized, it is not too absurd to see Una Merkel as an avenging angel of decent American womanhood (she had played Ann Rutledge to Walter Huston's Abe Lincoln), getting back at Marlene for all her Continental wiles by pulling Dietrich's hair. While *Destry* could thus be subtitled the Americanization of Marlene (we even see her gnawing on a porkchop), there is also a peculiarly Dietrichian sexual role-reversal to the climax. Whereas Bottleneck could not be reformed by its menfolk, Dietrich briefly associates with and leads the women in successful revolt, establishing law and order. For leaving the male world in which she is so much more comfortable, Frenchy is shot. If the song is to be believed, however, she would not wish either to be mourned or remembered as a woman among other women. "Just see what the boys in the back room will have . . .and tell them I died of the same."

Following the success of *Destry*, Dietrich had signed a contract to film *Bruges La Morte* in France with Raimu, whom she has referred to as "the greatest actor." With the outbreak of war and the French mobilization, the project was canceled.

Marlene remained in Hollywood and made *Seven Sinners* (1940) for Joe Pasternak. In many ways the film is a poor man's *Morocco* with a touch of *Camille*. Bijou is a character, not unlike Amy Jolly, who has run out of places in which she can hide from her past. With a change in governors she can return to the South Seas island of Boni-Komba and appear once again at Billy Gilbert's Café Seven Sinners. Director Tay Garnett reports in his *Light Your Torches and Pull up Your Tights* (Arlington House, 1973) on the selection of John Wayne as Dietrich's co-star. After the two actors were introduced, she looked Wayne up and down and told Garnett, "Daddy, buy me *that*." For Garnett *Seven Sinners* remains just a fun movie, and there is nothing in his unassuming autobiography to indicate that this may very well be the best of the fifteen films Dietrich made between *Desire* and *Stage Fright*.

Seven Sinners is lushly photographed by Rudolph Maté who had served his apprenticeship with Carl Dreyer, René Clair, and Fritz

SEVEN SINNERS (1940). With Broderick Crawford and Mischa Auer

Lang. The imagery of a Dietrich film had not been as sophisticated and complex since her parting with Sternberg. The exotic locale provided Garnett with the opportunity to play with light and shadow, foreground and background in a manner strikingly reminiscent of the master. Actually, in terms of plot, *Seven Sinners* is clearly derivative of Garnett's own *Her Man* (1930), a classic of the early sound era. *Her Man*, in fact, winds up in a brawl almost identical to the one which climaxes *Seven Sinners*.

Wayne, only one year but already nine films removed from *Stagecoach*, is extremely good with Diet-

SEVEN SINNERS (1940). With John Wayne at her right

rich, and they were to be paired twice more in 1942. Billy Gilbert and Oscar Homolka perform entertaining variations on the characters played by Paul Porcasi and Adolphe Menjou in *Morocco*, and Mischa Auer and Broderick Crawford offer strong comic support.

From her first throaty rendition of "I Can't Give You Anything But Love, Baby" on, Dietrich gives an impeccable performance. Bijou is much more introspective than Frenchy. Her vulnerability is more credible, and her irony more cutting. For all the chaos of the stuntman's paradise that it is, *Seven Sinners* has some remarkably

THE FLAME OF NEW ORLEANS (1941). With Bruce Cabot

human and poignant moments in its conventional tale of a tawdry café singer's abortive romance with a naval officer. Seldom has a movie seemingly so slight said so much about the improbability of happiness, about the ultimate and utter inadequacy of anything but love, baby. Even Dietrich's reversal of roles here has a less provocative quality. As she sings Hollander's "The Man's in the Navy" in a dashing white uniform, the tone is less mocking than respectful, less perverse than reverential. The implication is that Marlene's masquerade is

THE FLAME OF NEW ORLEANS (1941). With Roland Young

nothing more than that, that getting into a man's pants is a bit easier than assuming his persona. (Garnett's world is a very straight one, however Fordian or Hawksian it may be in the grace it allows those who are different.) Dietrich must finally lose her man to a nice dull girl who won't try to subsume him and his "shoulders, broad and glorious." Unlike Frenchy, Bijou is allowed to live, and one is left to presume that she and alcoholic doctor Albert Dekker will try to reform each other, at least until her ship reaches the next island.

THE FLAME OF NEW ORLEANS (1941). With Andy Devine
and Bruce Cabot

Dietrich's third and final film for Pasternak was *The Flame of New Orleans* (1941), René Clair's first American film. It is structured like Clair's masterpiece of a decade earlier, *Le Million*, in that it starts at the end and then flashes back to recount the events that have brought about such a bizarre conclusion. The plot has to do with a phony countess, a cross between the heroines of *Desire* and *Destry*, and her efforts to marry stodgy old Roland Young for his money. Her previous reputation catches up with her in the form of Mischa Auer who

MANPOWER (1941). With George Raft

recalls her Russian misadventures in St. Petersburg. In order to persuade Young and his aunt (Laura Hope Crews) that she is really a good girl, Dietrich assumes a second identity, that of her "bad" cousin who bears her a striking resemblance. Ultimately, as she is about to marry into Young's fortune, she gives in to her emotions and sails off with Bruce Cabot on his boat—her wedding dress thrown overboard, floating down the Mississippi, leaving Young to think that she has drowned.

Flame has lovely production values, reflecting Clair's retention of his craftsmanship long after he lost the inspiration of his early years. Unfortunately there are too many echoes and too much rehashing of Dietrich's recent films and the work of other directors. Chaplin's influence is evident in such scenes as the one in which a tightrope-walking Cabot comes a cropper because of a monkey (*The Circus*), and the one in which Dietrich fails to show up for the dinner he had meticulously prepared for her (*The Gold Rush*). Some of the slapstick seems borrowed from Clair's own *Italian Straw Hat*, and many of his civilized touches adorn the movie, but not enough.

Dietrich, despite a certain stiffness, holds the film together and almost makes its combined romanticism and romantic parody work.

Her flirting with Young recalls her manipulation of Edward Everett Horton in *The Devil Is a Woman*. The script by Norman Krasna is witty ("You don't catch men in Paris having the gout"), and Marlene's rendition of "Sweet As the Blush of May" is delightfully piquant. There is a delicious knowing quality about Crews' warnings to Dietrich, when she is about to be married to Young, about the baser aspect of man's nature: "Be brave." Unfortunately *The Flame of New Orleans* is too knowing, its ironies too felicitous, its charm too calculated. And no film can completely overcome the difficulty of having Bruce Cabot as the romantic lead, not even *King Kong*.

With *Manpower* (1941) and a move to Warner Bros., Dietrich makes her first appearance in a decade amidst contemporary American reality. Her Fay Duval, the soiled lady who becomes the point of contention between two tough power linesmen (Edward G. Robinson and George Raft), is a forerunner of the tough characters Joan Crawford would soon be playing at Warners, a creature more of iron than irony. Although her character is not terribly far removed from those of the Pasternak films, she never achieves the glitter of her predecessors, in or out of the saloon. *Manpower* also comes during director Raoul Walsh's strongest

MANPOWER (1941). With Edward G. Robinson

period (*The Roaring Twenties*, *They Drive By Night*, *High Sierra*, *Strawberry Blonde*, *They Died With Their Boots On*, *Gentleman Jim*) which makes it seem even slighter than it is. The Walshian adolescent humor provided by Alan Hale and Frank McHugh often is too intrusive, and Dietrich's absentee father's talking about the power cables ("They're treacherous as a snake . . . Devil's Fourth of July")

as though they were "dat ole davil sea" is a strained and inappropriate borrowing from Eugene O'Neill.

Robinson, who is billed ahead of Dietrich, essentially recreates sans Portuguese accent the role he played in Howard Hawks' much better *Tiger Shark* a decade earlier. His relationship with George Raft is the same as the one he shared with Richard Arlen in the Hawks film, and his physical infirmity caused by

THE LADY IS WILLING (1942). With Stanley Ridges and Aline MacMahon

his occupation (crippling by a hot wire here, the loss of a hand in *Tiger Shark*) results in a feeling of sexual inadequacy, Hollywood's way of skirting a castration complex. Dietrich (Zita Johann in the original) marries him out of affectionate boredom, but finding domesticated life even more tedious, begins to burn for Raft. All is ultimately cor-rected when Robinson obligingly is killed, but not before he bestows his blessings on them.

There is something unduly squalid about *Manpower*, beyond the necessities of milieu and symptomatic of Marlene's accumulating career problems. Whether she is spitting into her mascara box after emerging from jail or telling Raft "If

THE LADY IS WILLING (1942). With Fred MacMurray

I want to roll in the gutter, let me roll," one can sense that Dietrich, like Fay Duval, is in for hard times ahead. There is a bit too much reality in Eve Arden's bitchy "first few wrinkles you show, you're washed up." In spite of a cordial atmosphere on the set (Walsh allowed Marlene to participate in her lighting) and a competent performance, *Manpower* signaled a warning of a need for a new Dietrich and prompted some experimentation toward that end.

The Lady Is Willing (1942), like Dietrich's other Mitchell Leisen film *Golden Earrings*, is more in-teresting for its novelty than for any intrinsic value. This film made for Columbia, Marlene's third studio in a year, does not fit easily into any category. Dietrich's dabbling in domesticity had brought mixed results in *Blonde Venus* and *Manpower*. Here her motherhood—she "adopts" an abandoned infant—is in conflict with a booming stage career, highlighted by her appearance in what must be, judging by the finale which we see, the most ghastly musical comedy in the history of Broadway. Actually, *The Lady Is Willing* was hastily assembled as a project to

107

THE SPOILERS (1942). With John Wayne

THE SPOILERS (1942). With Richard Barthelmess

raise money for Marlene's forth-coming USO tour only when the plans for a movie on George Sand fell through.

Dietrich—even in modern dress and "the screwiest hat"—remains Dietrich. Her cajoling of pediatri-cian Fred MacMurray to come see her newly found baby, for example, is almost pure Concha Perez. And one wonders if there were autobio-graphical touches intended by hav-ing Marlene's platonic husband preoccupied with raising rabbits (Mr. Sieber is a chicken farmer) and separated from her by chicken wire when they have a falling out.

"She was the most fascinating woman who ever lived." This is Leisen's assessment of his star in David Chierichetti's book-length interview, *Hollywood Director*

(Curtis, 1973). Leisen goes on to call *The Lady Is Willing* one of Dietrich's best performances, certainly a forgivable exaggeration. It is surely one of her most accessible performances, full of humor, nose wiggling, and warmth. It is the performance of an actress who seems very doubtful about the nature and loyalty of her audience. Her big emotional scene with Fred MacMurray, finally expressing her love for him and her faith in his ability to save the baby's life, is played with Marlene's face firmly buried in his shoulder. This strange direction, whether the work of Leisen or Dietrich, is symbolic of the rather ill-defined and furtive quality of the star's persona at this stage of her career.

With the return to Universal and *The Spoilers*, Dietrich had come full cycle from the new beginning which *Destry Rides Again* had offered. Her Continental Mae West saloon girl had become as familiar as her thirties characters, and audiences would not pay to see her re-create the same role indefinitely. Symbolically, the film itself was the fourth version of the Rex Beach story; Ray Enright was the most forgettable director with whom she had worked since leaving Germany, and Randolph Scott was miscast as a villain. The Wayne-Dietrich pairing did not significantly rekindle the sparks of *Seven Sinners*, and there weren't even any songs for her to sing.

Some of the most interesting things in *The Spoilers* are on the fringes. This was, for example, the last film of Richard Barthelmess, probably the greatest silent actor America ever produced, who had become a star pining for Lillian Gish and who was now leaving the screen doing the same for Marlene Dietrich. In the same vein, William Farnum, star of the original 1914 version was brought back to play a supporting role. It was Farnum who had engaged with Tom Santschi in the endless climactic brawl (repeated here) which ostensibly occurred when Santschi miscalculated on the first punch and broke Farnum's nose. Coincidentally, the 1930 version was the film Gary Cooper made just before *Morocco*.

While *The Spoilers* was being shot, the Japanese were advancing across the Pacific and Dietrich's fellow Germans were crushing remaining resistance on the Continent. It must have become obvious to her that much more was happening in the world and to her adopted country than could be coped with on the Universal backlot. She was soon to rise to a role off-screen as magnificent in its way as any she had ever played for Sternberg.

Pittsburgh (1942), Dietrich's last starring role for Universal, is one of those war-effort movies, a genre which has invariably become dated more than almost any other. Of all the films made in Hollywood during World War II dealing with the contemporary crisis, only a handful have retained any vestige of greatness. Except for actual combat films like Hawks' *Air Force* and Ford's *They Were Expendable*, perhaps only *Casablanca* has a timeless quality to it. *Pittsburgh* has the typical air of being slapped together as a sugar-coated propaganda piece.

The plot coating has to do with a rivalry bordering on a love affair between John Wayne and Randolph Scott, twin Horatio Algers of coal mining. After rising from the pits to struggle over control of the mining industry and incidentally Dietrich (Josie Winters, self-styled "hunky"), all ends amicably in teamwork aimed at winning the war. Anticipating King Vidor's similar but more lavish *An American Romance* by two years, *Pittsburgh* alternates much documentary footage of mining and military production with its fictional scenes.

Eclectic director Lewis Seiler and his writers seem to have been under the influence of *Citizen Kane*. The film's flashback structure, Wayne's larger-than-life character, Charles "Pittsburgh"

WAR, WHORE, AND GYPSY

Markham, and his relationship with his stodgy wife all appear to be borrowed from the Welles masterpiece. Scott has a falling out with Wayne similar to Joseph Cotten's break with Charles Foster Kane when the latter became too crassly egocentric, and Frank Craven plays a character very much like Everett Sloane's Mr. Bernstein.

Dietrich disappears for long sections of *Pittsburgh*, the romantic aspects of the drama being at best secondary. For some reason, those scenes she does appear in seem terribly overscored. There is an unfortunate and unredeemed camp quality to the film (can one imagine Dietrich living in Pittsburgh in the first place?), not helped by writing like Wayne's speech to her: "I'm your kind of guy, see, and you're my kind of a gal. We were cut from the same chunk." She does her best, but *Pittsburgh* is probably Marlene's slightest film to that time.

In the thirties Dietrich had applied for American citizenship. In 1938 when her career in Hollywood appeared finished, she refused a lavish offer to return to Germany and make films for the Third Reich. Ultimately she preferred Joe Pasternak to Adolph Hitler. More than

PITTSBURGH (1942). With Randolph Scott and John Wayne

that, Dietrich had made a firm commitment, and with the spread of war, it seemed only natural to put her talents at the service of her new country's cause. For three long years she appeared in some five hundred performances before the Allied troops all over Europe and North Africa, singing, mind-reading, and playing the musical saw. It was, she said, "the only important thing I've ever done." Thus she received the Medal of Freedom in 1947 with great pride. With justifiable arrogance, she speaks of war in her *ABC* book (Doubleday, 1962): "If you haven't been in it, don't talk about it." The image of Dietrich singing "Lili Marlene" to homesick men on a remote battle-field or outpost has become an intrinsic part of her myth. A fragment of this glorious chapter in her career is captured in *Follow the Boys* (1944), featuring a sequence in which Orson Welles saws Marlene in half to the delight and astonishment of assembled troops.

During her stint with the military, Dietrich managed to take a short time off to appear in MGM's Arabian Nights fantasy, *Kismet* (1944). It was her first supporting role and although there was much publicity attached to her controversial nautch dance, the film did little to advance her career. "Gilded Dietrich," a picture spread in *Life*, demonstrated the process whereby Marlene's legs were covered with four coats of gold paint daily, ostensibly to enhance the erotic appeal of her performance as a "dancer." Actually, Jamilla the courtesan (censors prevented her being called harem queen) was such a thankless and uninteresting role, aside from her brief dance, that one can speculate that Dietrich's conception of her career potential at the time must have been very low.

The film itself (directed by William Dieterle) has occasionally spectacular color scenes, its sets sometimes recalling Eisenstein's *Alexander Nevsky*. Ronald Colman, King of the Beggars and Marlene's prize at the end, looked older than he actually was, too old for the swashbuckling romantic figure he is supposed to be. Dietrich lives under the protection of Edward Arnold but is kept from his advances by her unspecified connections with the Macedonians. At one point Arnold is so frustrated by her unwillingness to "dance" that he threatens to cut off her head even if he does lose Macedonia. Ultimately Arnold, lovable villain that he is, is killed, and Colman and Dietrich ride off together on horseback.

The conception of Dietrich's role is a rather cruel parody of her earlier excursions into exotica. Her costuming and makeup range from the ridiculous to the grotesque. She does her best to cope with the demands of the part, but aside from her dance, the demands generally consisted of languishing about, eating grapes in a suggestive manner. The whole enterprise could not be in more marked contrast to the rest

PITTSBURGH (1942). With Randolph Scott

FOLLOW THE BOYS (1944). With Orson Welles

of her wartime endeavors.

Martin Roumagnac (1946), released in America in 1948 as *The Room Upstairs*, took the place of the film Dietrich was unable to make in France in 1940. In this steamy melodrama, she plays a provincial whore who conceals her past from her lover, Jean Gabin. When he finally discovers her reputation, he kills her in anger, only to learn that she had been faithful to him. The plot has some elements of the Renoir-Zola *La Bête Humaine,* one of the best of Gabin's prewar films. Because of its content, the American release print had half an hour cut from it when it was finally shown here in 1948.

Since the film is not available for viewing, one can only speculate on its value from the reviews. Comment was not favorable, most critics being disappointed that such an

KISMET (1944). As Jamilla

KISMET (1944). With Edward Arnold

auspicious coupling as Dietrich and Gabin provided such a dreary result under Georges Lacombe's direction. Dietrich wound up scurrying back to America and, of all places, Paramount Pictures.

Golden Earrings (1947) was a commercial if not an artistic success, reestablishing Dietrich in Hollywood. She had been selected by director Mitchell Leisen over Paramount's objections. The ten films she had made in the decade since *Angel* had not persuaded the studio that she was no longer box-office poison. Gypsy Lydia is one of Dietrich's most curious creations, and since large sections of the screenplay were changed by her good friend Leisen, it is quite possible that Marlene contributed a great deal to the eccentric development of her character in the finished film. Dietrich even lived

KISMET (1944). With Ronald Colman

among Parisian gypsies for a time for research purposes.

The plot concerns Dietrich's efforts to get British officer Ray Milland out of Germany in 1939 with the formula for a poison gas. During the course of their bizarre adventures together, Milland is transformed into a gypsy in both appearance and finally in spirit. After the war, he goes back to live with Marlene in her wagon.

Many of the incidental things in the film are even sillier than the plot itself. In its attempts to impose an artifically exotic quality on Dietrich, *Golden Earrings* follows in the wake of *Kismet* and harks back to *The Garden of Allah*. Dietrich's sophisticated persona had become too familiar to be acceptable in the role of a primitive creature cooking stew in the woods, warding off evil spirits by spitting, and grotesquely

MARTIN ROUMAGNAC (1946) (U.S.: THE ROOM UPSTAIRS, 1948).
With Jean Gabin

scaling a fish in bed. At least in *Destry Rides Again*, that other attempt to fashion a new image, she was able to retain her ironic perspective on events. Innocence was not a credible quality in Dietrich, at least not in middle age.

Matters are not helped by Milland's overacting, perhaps a result of his Academy Award for *Lost Weekend* or perhaps because of his running disagreement with Dietrich. The Nazis and Gypsies are both from Central Casting which combined with Leisen's heavy-handed execution of the melodrama, makes *Golden Earrings* a kind of textbook case of what was wrong with so many Hollywood films of the forties. There is a last-minute attempt to be socially significant (one hesitates to blame writer Abraham Polonsky, but probably must), a love scene in which Milland and Dietrich reveal how they have each acquired the other's qualities,

GOLDEN EARRINGS (1947). As Lydia

GOLDEN EARRINGS (1947). With Ray Milland

showing that there can be a workable merger of the races and universal brotherhood. Fortunately there was no market for Dietrich to go on playing gypsies, and she was still confronted with the long-delayed task of establishing a viable identity for herself.

Both the careers of Dietrich and Greta Garbo were in a similar state of crisis and disarray in the early forties. Following the disastrous *Two-Faced Woman*, Garbo opted to sit out World War II, hoping that the return of the European market after the war would enable her to regain sufficient popularity to resume her career. It never happened. Dietrich, too, made only her supporting appearance in *Kismet* after she left Universal, otherwise devoting herself entirely to the war effort. In a certain sense, had the war not come along, Dietrich might have had to invent it. Her situation had been getting worse with each film, and none of the experimentation she tried in finding new roles for herself offered any real potential. Her first two postwar movies also provided no solution.

Salvation came through several strokes of genius for which Dietrich herself must surely receive a large measure of the credit. In effect, what Dietrich did, beginning with *A Foreign Affair*, was to re-create her career by re-creating herself. She indulged and exploited the various aspects of her personality and history which together constituted her myth. Like that other mythical creature, the phoenix, Dietrich was no stranger to the desert (vide *Morocco* and *The Garden of Allah*). And, like the phoenix, Dietrich

RETURN TO GERMANY

was able to emerge from wandering in her own personal desert totally reborn, but still totally Marlene Dietrich, only more so.

One of the salient facts about the actress was that she was German. It had conditioned her youth, molded her career, and, as the horrors of Nazism were played out on the world stage, made her emotionally mature in a way that is still insufficiently appreciated. As a German in the postwar world, she felt she carried with her a responsibility and purpose, and her contributions to *A Foreign Affair*, *Judgment at Nuremberg*, and *The Black Fox* must be viewed within this fundamentally serious context.

Billy Wilder's *A Foreign Affair* (1948) is on the whole anything but serious. James Agee commented on the "rotten taste" of its humor, and a movie which jokes about concentration camps and starvation deserves to be taken to task for its many lapses. At the same time, Dietrich is so good, more interesting than she had been for nearly a decade, that one doesn't wish to seem ungrateful.

She plays an ex-Nazi entertainer appearing at the Lorelei Cabaret beneath a shattered postwar Berlin. She is involved with John

A FOREIGN AFFAIR (1948). With John Lund

A FOREIGN AFFAIR (1948). With Gordon Jones and Millard Mitchell

Lund, an American officer who feeds his masochism with his guilt over associating with Dietrich. Congresswoman Jean Arthur descends from Iowa on an investigative mission, similar to Garbo's visit to Paris in *Ninotchka*, also written by Wilder and Charles Brackett, among others. The plot concerns Lund's attempts to conceal his relationship with Dietrich from Arthur by making the latter think he is infatuated with her. Ultimately Lund does fall for Arthur in one of Wilder's saccharine endings so out of keeping with the cynicism which has gone before.

Andrew Sarris has criticized Wilder for his cruelty toward Arthur

(this was her penultimate film), but even if she had been treated sympathetically instead of as a caricatured virginal ninny, the incredible competition Dietrich provides in a smaller part would probably have been too much for her. Dietrich's superiority was already ordained by the films of the thirties in which each appeared, the inevitable primacy of romanticism over relevancy, the intrinsic value of Sternberg over Capra. In any case, this poses a major problem for the film. Since Dietrich is supposed to be a villainess, the fact that she is so much more interesting and charismatic than anyone else is a major dramatic flaw.

A FOREIGN AFFAIR (1948). As Erika von Schluetow

JUDGMENT AT NUREMBERG (1961). With Virginia Christine and Spencer Tracy

Marlene's best number, "Black Market," in which she "sells her goods," is curiously reminiscent of the apple-selling song from *Morocco*. ("I've got so many toys—don't be bashful—step up, boys.") It is by Friedrich Hollander with whom she had not worked since *Manpower*. The song has a clear Brechtian quality, perhaps accounted for by the close-knit character of Hollywood's German community in which Brecht lived between 1941 and 1947. Dietrich's other two songs ("Want to Buy Some Illusions, Slightly Used?" and "Amidst the Ruins of Berlin") also make bitter points, political weltschmerz of an order seldom seen in the American cinema. Her character remains unredeemed in its self-

ishness, attempting to justify herself only with the assertion, "We Germans can't afford to be generous." Wilder, a former resident of Berlin himself, must ruthlessly show that naïve Americans can be easily corrupted by evil Germans, but ultimately good triumphs. An unrepentent Marlene is sent off to a labor camp. The ultimate irony is that Billy Wilder is the cinema's classic case of a naïve German corrupted by the cynicism and banality of America.

Dietrich's 1960 concert tour was remarkable in several ways. In April, despite published threats of a barrage of rotten tomatoes, she made her first public appearance in Germany since the thirties. She had helped the Allies to take Berlin in

JUDGMENT AT NUREMBERG (1961). With Spencer Tracy

1945 and before, during, and after the war had made remarks that could be considered not just anti-Nazi but anti-German. Her appearance in West Berlin under the auspices of Mayor Willy Brandt, however, was a triumph. Two months later in Jerusalem she broke the Israeli ban on the use of German language in a ten-day series of concerts, each of which was concluded with a half-hour standing ovation. In her book two years later she said of Israel: "There I washed my face in the cool water of compassion."

In 1961 Dietrich appeared in Stanley Kramer's *Judgment at Nuremberg* in a role which easily could be viewed as an extension of the one she played in *A Foreign Affair*. Whereas the Wilder film made light of carnage and adversity, Kramer imposed his typically humorless and styleless vision on many of the same issues. In *Judgment at Nuremberg* art is sacrificed to the cause of moralizing, the didactic points being hammered home in a long, often erratic exercise in courtroom tedium. Although Dietrich's character is a straw man with which Kramer brazenly manipulates his audience, Dietrich is once again so good, so much better than most of what surrounds her, that she tends to undermine the film's singularity of purpose.

In what is ultimately a small part within the context of a mammoth movie, Dietrich plays Frau Bertholt, the widow of an executed German general. Virtually all of her scenes are with Spencer Tracy who plays the judge at one of the Nuremberg trials. Her purpose is to persuade Tracy that her husband was not a Nazi, that one of the defendants interestingly named Ernst Janning (Burt Lancaster) was not a Nazi, and that the Germans "are not all monsters." When Tracy decides at the end of the film that Janning was culpable for the atrocities which are graphically illustrated with documentary footage, he is, in Dietrich's eyes, passing judgment on her. Kramer's point is that all Germans are guilty, regardless of any silent contempt they may have had for Hitler and the Nazis.

Tracy is one of the strongest actors with whom Dietrich ever worked, and, regardless of the material, it is a sheer pleasure to see these two relaxed professionals perform together. Their relationship in the film is warm, almost touching, and one is left to regret that they never had a chance to combine their talents before. There are some rare moments of poetry for a Kramer film in the scene where Tracy walks her home from a concert through the ruined streets of the city. On the sound track we hear "Lili Marlene" coming from a beerhall, and Dietrich joins in and explains the song to the American. She takes him home and makes coffee: "It's ersatz, but I always try to make it strong." She tells him of being brought up in a military family, a disciplined aristocratic heritage. After a while one begins to think that this is not Frau Bertholt, but someone else more familiar. It is, in fact, what Dietrich might have become if Josef von Sternberg had not seen the potential for Lola-Lola in an obscure young actress so long

JUDGMENT AT NUREMBERG (1961). At the trial

ago. She is telling the story of what might have been, and she is telling it with great presence and conviction.

The last shot of Dietrich—really the last shot of her film career to date—shows her sitting alone in the same apartment. Tracy has convicted Janning and the others; in effect, he has convicted all Germans for complicity in mass murder. He is calling Dietrich to say good-bye before returning to America. The phone is ringing, and there is a stunning closeup of Dietrich surrounded by shadow, refusing to answer. By agreeing to play this part in *Judgment at Nuremberg*, Dietrich is passing judgment herself on her fellow Germans, on what they became, and, indeed, on what she might have become.

Louis Clyde Stoumen's *The Black Fox* (1963) is very much in the spirit of *Judgment at Nuremberg*, holding the Germans responsible for what transpired during the Third Reich. Dietrich narrates this feature-length documentary which parallels Hitler's rise with Goethe's adaptation of the twelfth-century folktale, "Reynard the Fox." The concept recalls Brecht's *The Resistible Rise of Arturo Ui* which likens the Nazis to Chicago gangsters. In addition to newsreel footage, the film uses the art of Doré, Grosz, Picasso and others to illustrate its rather superficial points. The film has a tendency to only include those anti-German facts required to advance its argument, omitting, for example, the failed attempt to assassinate Hitler.

Although Dietrich cannot be blamed for the didacticism of *The Black Fox*, her reading itself is disappointingly stiff, only occasionally achieving the poignancy of which she is capable. One thinks of the great emotional range she attains in concert, for example, with "Where Have All the Flowers Gone?" Like *Judgment at Nuremberg*, *The Black Fox* was not a film calculated to increase Dietrich's popularity in Germany, but doubtless a film she felt she had to make. Since this may turn out to be her final movie (aside from her walk-on in *Paris When It Sizzles*, 1964), it is fitting that it should contain a still of Lola-Lola used to illustrate the flourishing of the arts in the Weimar Republic.

After a one-line appearance in *Jigsaw* (1949), in which she played a patron at the Blue Angel nightclub, Dietrich went to England to star in Alfred Hitchcock's *Stage Fright* (1950). Although *Stage Fright* pales somewhat by comparison with the great Hitchcock masterpieces which followed it (*Strangers on a Train*, *Rear Window*, *Vertigo*, *North By Northwest*, *Psycho*), it did offer Dietrich the opportunity to return to the grandly elegant style of her pre-war Paramount performances. There were also sufficient autobiographical connotations to the role of Charlotte Inwood to help establish the legend of Marlene as a great lady of the theater. In her *ABC* book, Dietrich says of arrogance: "On some people, it looks good." She must have had Charlotte Inwood in mind.

Hitchcock has indicated that what appealed to him in the project was its concern with the theater, particularly the relationship between acting novice Jane Wyman and star Marlene Dietrich, a similar relationship to that shared by Anne Baxter and Bette Davis in another 1950 film, *All About Eve*. Both women are ostensibly rivals for Richard Todd, the film's rather weak villain, on the run for killing Marlene's husband. The plot is too convoluted to go into, but significantly Dietrich rises above it to give

RETURN TO THE SALON

one of her most sustained and multi-layered performances.

She is marvelously perverse trying on a mourning gown and commenting: "This is very nice . . . but isn't there some way we could let it plunge a little in front?" She has a very ironic, perhaps very Dietrichian attitude toward her public. Her musical numbers ("Laziest Girl in Town" and "La Vie En Rose") have a stately elegance which clearly anticipates the concert appearances she was soon to make, into which both of these songs were to be incorporated. When called upon to cope with dramatic moments, such as the scene in which she is publicly confronted with a blood-stained doll indicating that her involvement in the murder is known, she is masterful. When she is tricked by Wyman into confessing, Dietrich's big moment of introspection is brought off with considerable effect, culminating in a devastating closeup. All in all, *Stage Fright* permitted Dietrich to play a larger-than-life woman similar to herself, more mature now but still possessing a stately and sensual allure. Beneath the harsh exterior, one senses a vulnerable and very real human being.

STAGE FRIGHT (1950). With Jane Wyman

Dietrich remained in England and was reunited with James Stewart in Henry Koster's *No Highway in the Sky* (1951). Her character, screen actress Monica Teasdale, once again suggests autobiography. Stewart plays the eccentric Mr. Honey, a caricatured absentminded scientist something along the lines of Cary Grant in *Bringing Up Baby*. Honey becomes convinced that the airliner in which both he and Dietrich are flying is about to come apart in the air. He tries to persuade her and others on board, including stewardess Glynis Johns, that his assessment is correct. Although the plane does not crash, he is ultimately vindicated.

No Highway is a very talky movie, visually closer to a television drama. Actually, one or two of Dietrich's scenes seem more carefully lit than the others, and one senses she may have had a hand in this. The plot is loaded with improbabilities, and Stewart's central character is too broadly drawn. Once again he and Marlene play nicely together in roles far removed from *Destry Rides Again*.

One is very tempted to read Dietrich autobiographical inferences into Teasdale's musings over her career, her life, and her death. Stewart, in the process of informing her of the impending crash, tells her of the importance of her films to him and his late wife. She responds with a cynical reference to "a few cans of celluloid in a junk heap someday." She goes on to talk about her reluc-

STAGE FRIGHT (1950).
With Richard Todd

NO HIGHWAY IN THE SKY (1951). With Glynis Johns and James Stewart

NO HIGHWAY IN THE SKY (1951). With Jack Hawkins and Ronald Squire

THE MONTE CARLO STORY (1957). With Vittorio De Sica

tance to retire because she's never
been able to figure out what to do
with herself. She speculates on all
the people who will come to her
funeral: "That'll be quite an occasion." She cries when Stewart tells
her that he and his wife never walk-
ed out on any of her films. It is a

self-conscious performance, but
like her even more self-conscious
concert performances, Dietrich
brings it off with style.

The Monte Carlo Story (1957) is
Desire twenty years later, with all
the champagne gone flat. (Italian
star Renato Rascel plays Duval the

WITNESS FOR THE PROSECUTION (1957). At the trial, with Tyrone Power in the dock and the lawyers (including Charles Laughton) conferring

jeweler, probably an explicit *hommage* to *Desire*.) Dietrich and Vittorio De Sica are adventurers who, believing the other has money, wind up married and disillusioned to discover they are both broke. After Dietrich has a fling with wealthy American Arthur O'Connell and De Sica with O'Connell's daughter (Natalie Trundy), the two stars reconcile themselves to being happily poor together.

Perhaps George Cukor might have been imaginative enough to make this color and widescreen production work. Samuel A. Taylor shoots uninteresting long takes, and his lighting is at best unflattering. The archness of Dietrich's performance is accentuated by the banality and witlessness of the dialogue, and De Sica's charm is lost in his struggle with English. The film is a fairly obvious attempt to do for Marlene what David Lean's *Summertime* did for Katharine Hepburn. Instead, it is something of an embarrassment, a film that even Mr. Honey and his wife would find it hard to sit through.

Witness For the Prosecution

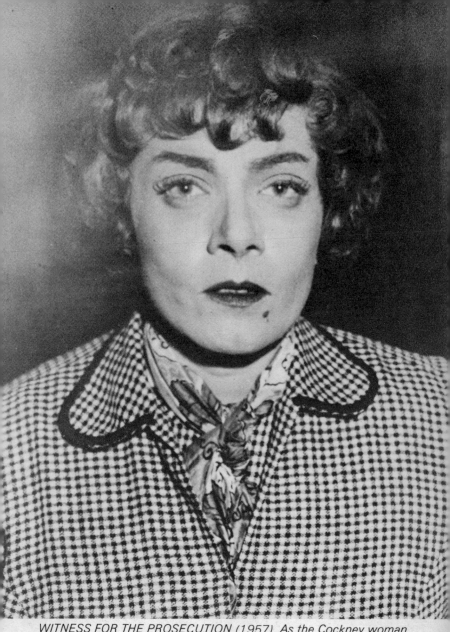

WITNESS FOR THE PROSECUTION (1957). As the Cockney woman

(1957) owes much to *Stage Fright* (and other Hitchcock films, notably *The Paradine Case*) and should have borrowed more. The relationship between Dietrich and Tyrone Power (his last completed film) has many of the same qualities she shared with Richard Todd in the earlier film. Although both films are often verbose to the point of boredom, Billy Wilder's whodunit offers none of the splendid Hitchcockian set-pieces to periodically spark interest. Instead, Wilder relies on the considerable talents of his actors (Charles Laughton is superb) to carry him through. The company includes such Hitchcock regulars as John Williams and Norma Varden in supporting roles. Acting is not really enough to overcome Wilder's stylistic inadequacy, however, and *Witness* pales by comparison with the visual fluidity of a similar project like Preminger's *Anatomy of a Murder*.

Although Dietrich arrives late in the film and has only about a half dozen scenes, she contests Laughton for predominance. Wilder evokes Marlene's past and their previous collaboration on *A Foreign Affair* with a flashback to a German cabaret where she first meets Power and loses half her pants. Marlene's famous cockney imitation is a tour de force, although one can detect the slight rolling of the "r's" characteristic of her speech. Unfortunately, this gimmick took some of the focus off what was certainly one of her best postwar performances. By 1957 it was increasingly difficult to determine where the role playing left off and the real Dietrich began. As Laughton understates, at the film's end, she is "a remarkable woman."

Rancho Notorious (1952) re-creates the third and most familiar part of the Marlene myth, the Dietrich of *The Blue Angel*, *Morocco*, *Destry Rides Again*, and *Seven Sinners*. The project was conceived by Fritz Lang and writer Daniel Taradash specifically for her, and throughout there is a conscious evocation of the legend which began with Lola-Lola. The film is framed by Ken Darby's "Chuck-a-Luck" song. (*Chuck-a-Luck* was Lang's original title for the film before Howard Hughes arbitrarily changed it.) Lang had already experimented with this kind of Brechtian device in *You and Me* (1938). We first see Dietrich in flashback ("she was a glory gal in those days"), cigarette and beer at the ready, her foot up on a chair in her traditional manner. Although Lang is ostensibly showing us a series of flashbacks on the career of Altar Keane, no attempt is made to conceal the fact that he is also flashing back on the career of Marlene Dietrich.

Had Dietrich's Frenchy survived *Destry*, there might very well have come a time when she would have settled down on her own Chuck-a-Luck Ranch and made it a haven for desperadoes. One can easily imagine her sitting around the piano, cigarette dangling erotically from her mouth, singing "Get Away, Young Man, Get Away" to her "house guests." Arthur Ken-

RETURN TO THE SALOON

nedy, playing a vengeance-bent cowboy, comments that he once thought that she might be only a legend, and Dietrich reassures him that she is no "pipe dream." There is a bit of business in which Marlene refuses to discuss her age. She tells Kennedy she wishes he'd go away and come back ten years ago, echoing precisely what Gary Cooper had told her in *Morocco*. She says of him, "He makes you remember yourself a long time back." Ultimately, Dietrich is shot dead as she was in *Destry*, shielding the man she loves.

Part of the problem with *Rancho Notorious* has to do with its low budget. The film is almost entirely studio-made, and painted backdrops are much harder to accept in westerns and other action genres than elsewhere. Lang's themes of "hate, murder, and revenge" are imposed a bit heavy-handedly on the material, and some of the casting is less than perfect. The style is subdued by Lang's standards, and the color photography works against his visual strength, his effective use of darkness and shadow in films like *M* and *The Big Heat*. It is hard to have a *film noir* in garish Technicolor.

RANCHO NOTORIOUS
(1952). As Altar Keene

RANCHO NOTORIOUS (1952). With Mel Ferrer

In his book-length interview with Peter Bogdanovich (*Fritz Lang in America*, Praeger, 1969), Lang is very bitter toward Dietrich. Although her performance is quite good and although the film is clearly constructed around her, Dietrich was very unhappy during the course of production. According to Lang, she resented the implications of her character which suggested she was past her prime, and invoked Sternberg's ideas on directing and lighting to contradict his own. In defense of Dietrich, one is compelled to point out that Lang has frequently been in conflict with his collaborators, whereas, with the exception of Selznick, Marlene generally received praise from her mentors for her cooperative attitude.

In any case, *Rancho Notorious* ranks with Dietrich's most interesting postwar films, and, however she may have received it, it is a gesture toward preserving and revivifying an important aspect of the international institution known as Marlene Dietrich.

Although *Rancho Notorious* prompted a cover article in *Life* on "Dietrich and Her Magic Myth," she did not make another film for four years. Her cameo in Mike Todd's *Around the World in Eighty Days* (1956) can hardly be considered an important contribution to her legend. She is once again a Wild

139

TOUCH OF EVIL (1958). With Orson Welles

West saloon girl, reunited with George Raft of *Manpower* as her jealous boyfriend. Marlene has a somewhat embalmed look in her garishly lit scene in Clancy's bar, anticipating the poor photography she received the following year in *The Monte Carlo Story*. David Niven comes into the saloon in search of his butler, Cantinflas. He tells Dietrich he is looking for "my man" to which she responds suggestively, "So am I."

A more positive evocation of Dietrich's past comes in Orson Welles' *Touch of Evil* (1958). There is more than a touch of sad irony to the fact that in the best of all

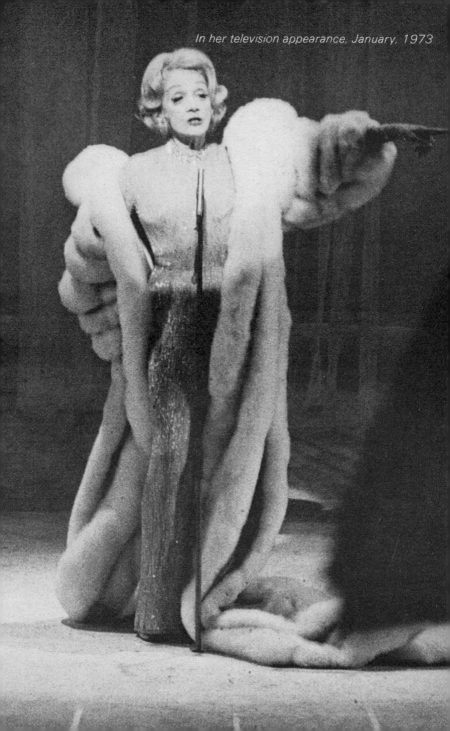

In her television appearance, January, 1973

In her television appearance, January, 1973

those films she made after the separation from Sternberg, she should appear for only a few minutes. Space does not permit a full discussion of those qualities which make *Touch of Evil* one of the most superb creations of one of the screen's greatest masters.

Welles, who must continually confront his own legend, has a clear understanding of the myth of his old friend Marlene. Her character of Tanya, the gypsy-like, cigar-smoking, fortune-telling madam, is built around his conception of these mythic qualities. When, in the person of Hank Quinlan, Welles crosses the border into Mexico and hears Tanya's pianola, he marvels that she's "still open for business." The border town itself evokes the sordidness of the waterfront street which long ago harbored the Blue Angel cabaret. Dietrich appears but does not at first recognize her old friend in the mountainous man before her: "You should lay off those candy bars . . . you're a mess, honey." She warns Hank that her "chili" may now be too hot for him.

As Detective Quinlan, caught in an illegal act, disintegrates, he goes back to Tanya's for solace and reflection on the happier, more innocent past they shared. He asks to have his fortune read, and Dietrich tells him his "future's all used up." Finally, when Quinlan is ensnared

and shot, dying in a pool of muddy water, Tanya eulogizes: "He was some kind of a man. What does it matter what you say about people?"

Dietrich's part in *Touch of Evil* is small only in terms of screen time. Yet in only a few minutes she gives one of the most memorable and moving performances of her career. She herself said recently, "I've never been as good as I was in that little teensy part." *Touch of Evil*, like the Sternberg films, both elicits and enhances the magic and mystery that is Marlene.

Now we all might enjoy seeing Helen of
   Troy as a gay cabaret entertainer,
But I doubt that she could be one quarter as good as our legendary, lovely
   Marlene.

                                    Noël Coward

In the four years which separated *Rancho Notorious* from *Around the World in Eighty Days*, Dietrich embarked on her still-flourishing career as a live performer. Beginning in 1953 at the Hotel Sahara (shades of her American film debut in *Morocco*) in Las Vegas and then moving the following year to the Café de Paris in London, Dietrich sang the songs associated with her life and legend, from "Falling in Love Again" to "Lili Marlene." It was not long before she moved her act to the more refined atmosphere of the legitimate theater, away from the sordidness of clinking glasses and bubbling bottles, the milieu

Performing her night club act

from which Lola-Lola had first emerged. By 1959 (the year she was feted at the Museum of Modern Art to open a retrospective of her films), she had also begun a radio program in which she offered practical advice on "love and life," and her record albums were selling in vast quantities around the world.

In 1967 and 1968, Dietrich's by now meticulously streamlined show was brought to Broadway for two highly successful runs, the second billing her as "The Queen of the World." In addition to her standard repertoire, she offered her commentary on Vietnam in a moving rendition of "Where Have All the Flowers Gone?" One critic has perceptively commented on the ironic quality of these performances. It is as though Dietrich were looking over her own shoulder and examining her image and her legend with some degree of detachment and amusement.

Dietrich on stage has been subjected to criticism for the too-perfect control, the overt artifice of the ceremonial rite which her show seems to the unsympathetic. To view her performances as evocation rather than embalmment, one does require perhaps some knowledge of her career, some respect for her myth, and some imagination. Her very Prussian preciseness (which Dietrich once referred to as a key to her character) and her need to play away from the more cloying tendencies of other artists have always imposed a certain remoteness on her relationship with her audience.

As with Amy Jolly walking into the desert, a full appreciation of the live Dietrich demands partial suspension of disbelief, a willingness to grant special qualities to someone who defiantly claims to be and is in fact larger than life. Because of this, it is not surprising that Dietrich's long-delayed television debut in 1973 did not please even some of her devoted admirers. The electric atmosphere of the stage is lost when Dietrich's image is squeezed through the tiny electronic box. In the theater, as Sternberg said of his mise-en-scène, "the very air becomes part of the effect."

And so she goes on. She recently celebrated her fiftieth wedding anniversary, and *Variety* informs us that she and Rudi have incorporated. After her 1973 fall from a Maryland stage, her January 1974 concert series at Carnegie Hall had to be canceled. Since the resumption of her tour, she has continued to relive her life before her audience like a contemporary Lola Montes, continued to offer up her memories and conjure up those she shares with the multitude which remembers and comes to see her. There is an unverified story that the reason Dietrich refuses to retire has to do with the serious illness of someone very close to her, a plot right out of *Blonde Venus*. There is also a report from Normandy that she has just purchased her own gravesite, convenient to a charming restaurant where her friends can have lunch when they visit. There is also no doubt that Marlene will be with us forever, that she is immortal if for no other reason than, as Joe Pasternak said of her, "perfection is ageless." She will surely never die—but when she dies, don't pay the preacher for speaking of her glory and her fame—just see what the boys in the back room will have. . . .

BIBLIOGRAPHY

Aherne, Brian. *A Proper Job.* Houghton, Mifflin, Boston, 1969.

Behlmer, Rudy (ed.). *Memo From: David O. Selznick.* Avon, New York, 1972.

Bogdanovich, Peter. "Encounters with Josef von Sternberg." *Movie,* #13 (Summer, 1965).

——————. *Fritz Lang in America.* Praeger, New York, 1969.

Bowers, Ronald L. "Marlene Dietrich: '54-70." *Films in Review,* Vol. XXII, #1, (Jan., 1971)

Bowser, Eileen (ed.). *Film Notes.* The Museum of Modern Art, New York, 1969.

Carr, Larry. *Four Fabulous Faces.* Arlington House, New Rochelle, 1970.

Chierichetti, David. *Hollywood Director: The Career of Mitchell Leisen.* Curtis, New York, 1973.

Corliss, Richard. *Talking Pictures.* Overlook, New York, 1974.

Dickens, Homer. *The Films of Marlene Dietrich.* Citadel, New York, 1968.

Dietrich, Marlene. *Marlene Dietrich's ABC.* Doubleday, Garden City, 1962.

Frewin, Leslie. *Dietrich: The Story of a Star.* Avon, New York, 1972.

Georg, Manfred. *Marlene Dietrich.* Ralph A. Höger Verlag, Berlin, 1931.

Griffith, Richard. *Marlene Dietrich: Image and Legend.* The Museum of Modern Art, New York, 1959.

Hervey, Harry. *Shanghai Express.* Treatment available for study at the Film Study Center, the Museum of Modern Art.

Hessell, Franz. *Marlene Dietrich.* Kindt und Bucher Verlag, Berlin, 1931.

Hughes, Elinor. *Famous Stars of Filmdom.* L.C. Page, Boston, 1931.

Kobal, John. *Marlene Dietrich.* Dutton, New York, 1968.

Koszarski, Richard. "Jules Furthman," in *The Hollywood Screenwriters* (ed. by Richard Corliss). Avon, New York, 1972.

Lasserre, Jean. *La Vie Brûlante de Marlene Dietrich.* Nouvelle Librairie Francaise, Paris, 1931.

Milne, Tom. *Rouben Mamoulian.* Indiana University Press, Bloomington, 1969.

Pasternak, Joe. *Easy the Hard Way.* Putnam, New York, 1956.

Rheuban, Joyce. "Josef von Sternberg: the Scientist and the Vamp." *Sight and Sound,* V. 42, #1 (Winter 1972-3).

Sarris, Andrew. *The Films of Josef von Sternberg.* The Museum of Modern Art, New York, 1966.

Silver, Charles. "A Love Letter to Marlene." *Classic Film Collector* (Spring, 1968).

——————. "Sternberg: In Memoriam." *The Village Voice* (January 8, 1970).

Sternberg, Josef von. *The Blue Angel.* (authorized translation of the German continuity). Simon and Schuster, New York, 1968.

——————. *Fun in a Chinese Laundry.* Macmillan, New York, 1965.

——————. *Morocco* and *Shanghai Express* (scripts). Simon and Schuster, New York, 1973.

Tabori, Paul. *Alexander Korda.* Osbourne, London, 1959.

Weinberg, Herman, *Josef von Sternberg.* Dutton, New York, 1967.

——————. *The Lubitsch Touch.* Dutton, New York, 1968.

Weisstein, Ulrich. "Professor Unrat and The Blue Angel." *Film Journal,* V. I, #3-4 (Fall-Winter 1972).

THE FILMS OF MARLENE DIETRICH

The director's name follows the release date. A (c) following the release date indicates that the film is in color. Sp indicates Screenplay and b/o indicates based/on.

Silent Period

1. DER KLEINE NAPOLEON (THE LITTLE NAPOLEON). 1923. *Georg Jacoby.*

2. TRAGÖDIE DER LIEBE (TRAGEDY OF LOVE). 1923. *Joe May.*

3. DER MENSCH AM WEGE (MAN BY THE ROADSIDE). 1923. *Wilhelm Dieterle.*

4. DER SPRUNG INS LEBEN (THE LEAP INTO LIFE). 1924. *Dr. Johannes Guter.*

5. DIE FREUDLOSE GASSE (JOYLESS STREET). 1925. *Georg Wilhelm Pabst.*

6. MANON LESCAUT. 1926. *Arthur Robison.*

7. EINE DU BARRY VON HEUTE (A MODERN DU BARRY). 1926. *Alexander Korda.*

8. MADAME WÜNSCHT KEINE KINDER (MADAME DOESN'T WANT CHILDREN). 1926. *Alexander Korda.*

9. KOPF HOCH, CHARLY! (HEADS UP, CHARLY!). 1926. *Dr. Willi Wolff.*

10. DER JUXBARON (THE IMAGINARY BARON). 1927. *Dr. Willi Wolff.*

11. SEIN GRÖSSTER BLUFF (HIS GREATEST BLUFF). 1927. *Harry Piel.*

12. CAFE ELECTRIC. 1927. *Gustav Ucicky.*

13. PRINZESSIN OLALA (PRINCESS OLALA). 1928. *Robert Land.*

14. ICH KÜSSE IHRE HAND, MADAME (I KISS YOUR HAND, MADAME). 1929. *Robert Land*.

15. DIE FRAU, NACH DER MAN SICH SEHNT (THE WOMAN ONE LONGS FOR). 1929. *Kurt Bernhardt*.

16. DAS SCHIFF DER VERLORENEN MENSCHEN (THE SHIP OF LOST SOULS). 1929. *Maurice Tourneur*.

17. GEFAHREN DER BRAUTZEIT (DANGERS OF THE ENGAGEMENT PERIOD). 1929. *Fred Sauer*.

Sound Period

18. DER BLAUE ENGEL (THE BLUE ANGEL). UFA, 1929. *Josef von Sternberg*. Sp: Josef von Sternberg, Robert Liebmann, Carl Zuckmayer, and Karl Vollmöller b/o novel *Professor Unrat* by Heinrich Mann. Cast: Emil Jannings, Kurt Gerron, Rosa Valetti, Hans Albers, Reinhold Bernt, Karl Huszar-Puffy, Rolf Muller. Remade in 1959.

19. MOROCCO. Paramount, 1930. *Josef von Sternberg*. Sp: Josef von Sternberg and Jules Furthman b/o novel *Amy Jolly* by Benno Vigny. Cast: Gary Cooper, Adolphe Menjou, Ulrich Haupt, Eve Southern, Paul Porcasi, Francis Mac-Donald, Juliette Compton, Albert Conti, Michael Visaroff, Emile Chautard.

20. DISHONORED. Paramount, 1931. *Josef von Sternberg*. Sp: Josef von Sternberg and Daniel N. Rubin, b/o story "X27" by Sternberg. Cast: Victor McLaglen, Lew Cody, Gustav von Seyffertitz, Warner Oland, Barry Norton, Davison Clark, Wilfred Lucas.

21. SHANGHAI EXPRESS. Paramount, 1932. *Josef von Sternberg*. Sp. Josef von Sternberg and Jules Furthman, b/o story by Harry Hervey. Cast: Clive Brook, Anna May Wong, Warner Oland, Eugene Pallette, Lawrence Grant, Louise Closser Hale, Gustav von Seyffertitz, Emile Chautard. Remade in 1951 as *Peking Express*.

22. BLONDE VENUS. Paramount, 1932. *Josef von Sternberg*. Sp: Josef von Sternberg, Jules Furthman, and S.K. Lauren, b/o story by Sternberg. Cast: Herbert Marshall, Cary Grant, Dickie Moore, Gene Morgan, Rita LaRoy, Robert Emmett O'Connor, Sidney Toler, Cecil Cunningham, Sterling Holloway, Hattie McDaniel, Emile Chautard.

23. SONG OF SONGS. Paramount, 1933. *Rouben Mamoulian*. Sp: Leo Birinski and Samuel Hoffenstein, b/o novel by Hermann Sudermann and play by Edward Sheldon. Cast: Brian Aherne, Lionel Atwill, Alison Skipworth, Hardie Albright, Helen Freeman.

24. **THE SCARLET EMPRESS**. Paramount, 1934. *Josef von Sternberg*. Sp: Josef von Sternberg and Manuel Komroff, b/o diary of Catherine the Great. Cast: John Lodge, Sam Jaffe, Louise Dresser, Maria Sieber, C. Aubrey Smith, Ruthelma Stevens, Olive Tell, Gavin Gordon, Jane Darwell, Jameson Thomas, Davison Clark.

25. **THE DEVIL IS A WOMAN**. Paramount, 1935. *Josef von Sternberg*. Sp: Josef von Sternberg and John Dos Passos, b/o novel *The Woman and the Puppet* by Pierre Louys, Cast: Lionel Atwill, Cesar Romero, Edward Everett Horton, Alison Skipworth, Don Alvarado, Morgan Wallace, Lawrence Grant, Tempe Pigott, Hank Mann, Jill Dennett. Also filmed in 1920 and 1958.

26. **DESIRE**. Paramount, 1936. *Frank Borzage*. Sp: Edwin Justus Mayer, Waldemar Young, Samuel Hoffenstein, b/o play by Hans Szekely and R.A. Stemmle. Cast: Gary Cooper, John Halliday, William Frawley, Ernest Cossart, Alan Mowbray, Zeffie Tilbury, Akim Tamiroff, Marc Lawrence.

27. **THE GARDEN OF ALLAH**, Selznick-International, 1936. (c) *Richard Boleslawski*. Sp: Willis Goldbeck, W.P. Lipscomb, Lynn Riggs, b/o novel by Robert Hichens. Cast: Charles Boyer, Basil Rathbone, Joseph Schildkraut, C. Aubrey Smith, Tilly Losch, John Carradine, Lucile Watson, Henry Brandon, Alan Marshall.

28. **KNIGHT WITHOUT ARMOUR**. Alexander Korda-London Films, 1937. *Jacques Feyder*. Sp: Frances Marion, Lajos Biro, and Arthur Wimperis b/o novel *Without Armour* by James Hilton. Cast: Robert Donat, Irene Vanbrugh, Herbert Lomas, Austin Trevor, Basil Gill, David Tree, John Clements, Hay Petrie, Miles Malleson, Dorice Fordred.

29. **ANGEL**. Paramount, 1937. *Ernst Lubitsch*. Sp: Samson Raphaelson, b/o play by Melchior Lengyel. Cast: Herbert Marshall, Melvyn Douglas, Edward Everett Horton, Laura Hope Crews, Ernest Cossart, Herbert Mundin, Ivan Lebedeff, Dennie Moore, Louise Carter.

30. **DESTRY RIDES AGAIN**. Universal, 1939. *George Marshall*. Sp: Felix Jackson, Gertrude Purcell, and Henry Myers, b/o novel by Max Brand. Cast: James Stewart, Charles Winninger, Una Merkel, Irene Hervey, Brian Donlevy, Jack Carson, Mischa Auer, Warren Hymer, Allen Jenkins, Lillian Yarbo. Previously filmed in 1932 and remade in 1950 as *Destry*.

31. **SEVEN SINNERS**. Universal, 1940, *Tay Garnett*. Sp: John Meehan and Harry Tugend, b/o story by Ladislaus Fodor and Lazlo Vadnay. Cast: John Wayne, Albert Dekker, Oscar Homolka, Billy Gilbert, Anna Lee, Mischa Auer, Broderick Crawford, Samuel S. Hinds, Reginald Denny, Vince Barnett, Antonio Moreno. Remade in 1954 as *South Sea Sinner*.

32. THE FLAME OF NEW ORLEANS. Universal, 1941. *René Clair*. Sp: Norman Krasna. Cast: Bruce Cabot, Roland Young, Mischa Auer, Andy Devine, Franklin Pangborn, Laura Hope Crews, Eddie Quillan, Frank Jenks, Theresa Harris, Anne Revere, Melville Cooper.

33. MANPOWER. Warner Brothers, 1941. *Raoul Walsh*. Sp: Richard Macauley and Jerry Wald. Cast: Edward G. Robinson, George Raft, Alan Hale, Frank McHugh, Eve Arden, Barton MacLane, Joyce Compton, Ward Bond, Egon Brecher, Barbara Pepper.

34. THE LADY IS WILLING. Columbia, 1942. *Mitchell Leisen*. Sp: James Edward Grant and Albert McCleery, b/o story by Grant. Cast: Fred MacMurray, Aline MacMahon, Stanley Ridges, Arline Judge, Roger Clark, Marietta Canty, Sterling Holloway, David James.

35. THE SPOILERS. Universal, 1942. *Ray Enright*. Sp: Lawrence Hazard and Tom Reed, b/o novel by Rex Beach. Cast: John Wayne, Randolph Scott, Richard Barthelmess, Harry Carey, Margaret Lindsay, George Cleveland, Samuel S. Hinds, Russell Simpson, William Farnum, Marietta Canty. Previously filmed in 1914, 1923, and 1930 and remade in 1955.

36. PITTSBURGH. Universal, 1942. *Lewis Seiler*. Sp: Kenneth Gamet and Tom Reed b/o story by Reed and George Owen. Cast: John Wayne, Randolph Scott, Frank Craven, Louise Allbritton, Shemp Howard, Thomas Gomez, Ludwig Stossel, Samuel S. Hinds.

38. FOLLOW THE BOYS. Universal, 1944. *Edward Sutherland*. Sp: Lou Breslow and Gertrude Purcell. Cast: George Raft, Vera Zorina, Grace McDonald, Charley Grapewin, Orson Welles, W.C. Fields.

38. KISMET. Metro-Goldwyn-Mayer, 1944. (c) *William Dieterle*. Sp: John Meehan, b/o play by Edward Knoblock. Cast: Ronald Colman, Edward Arnold, Hugh Herbert, Joy Ann Page, James Craig, Florence Bates, Harry Davenport, Hobart Cavanaugh, Charles Middleton. Previously filmed in 1920 and 1930 and remade as a musical in 1955.

39. MARTIN ROUMAGNAC (THE ROOM UPSTAIRS). Alcina, 1946. *Georges Lacombe*. Sp: Pierre Very, b/o novel by Pierre-René Wolf. Cast: Jean Gabin, Jean d'Yd, Margo Lion, Daniel Gelin, Marcel Herrand, Jean Darcante, Henri Poupon.

40. GOLDEN EARRINGS. Paramount, 1947. *Mitchell Leisen*. Sp: Abraham Polonsky, Frank Butler, Helen Deutsch, b/o novel by Yolanda Foldes. Cast: Ray Milland, Murvyn Vye, Bruce Lester, Dennis Hoey, Reinhold Schunzel, Quentin Reynolds, Ivan Triesault.

41. A FOREIGN AFFAIR. Paramount, 1948. *Billy Wilder*. Sp: Billy Wilder, Charles Brackett, and Richard Breen b/o story by David Shaw. Cast: Jean Arthur, John Lund, Millard Mitchell, Peter Von Zerneck, William Murphy, Stanley Prager.

42. JIGSAW. United Artists, 1949. *Fletcher Markle*. Sp: Fletcher Markle and Vincent McConnor, b/o story by John Roeburt. Cast: Franchot Tone, Jean Wallace, Myron McCormick, Marc Lawrence. Dietrich had walk-on.

43. STAGE FRIGHT. Warner Brothers, 1950. *Alfred Hitchcock*. Sp: Whitfield Cook, b/o novel *Man Running* by Selwyn Jepson. Cast: Jane Wyman, Alistair Sim, Richard Todd, Michael Wilding, Joyce Grenfell, Kay Walsh, Dame Sybil Thorndike, Miles Malleson, Hector MacGregor, Patricia Hitchcock.

44. NO HIGHWAY IN THE SKY. Twentieth Century-Fox, 1951. *Henry Koster*. Sp: Robert C. Sheriff, Oscar Millard, Alec Coppel, b/o novel by Nevil Shute. Cast: James Stewart, Glynis Johns, Jack Hawkins, Elizabeth Allan, Ronald Squire, Janette Scott, Niall McGinnis, Kenneth More, Wilfrid Hyde-White.

45. RANCHO NOTORIOUS. RKO-Radio, 1952. (c) *Fritz Lang*. Sp: Daniel Taradash, b/o story by Sylvia Richards. Cast: Arthur Kennedy, Mel Ferrer, William Frawley, Lloyd Gough, Gloria Henry, Lisa Ferraday, Jack Elam, Dan Seymour, Fuzzy Knight, John Doucette, Frank Ferguson, George Reeves.

46. AROUND THE WORLD IN 80 DAYS. United Artists, 1956. (c) *Michael Anderson*. Sp: S.J. Perelman, James Poe, and John Farrow b/o novel by Jules Verne. Cast: David Niven, Cantinflas, Robert Newton, Shirley MacLaine, George Raft, Frank Sinatra, Beatrice Lillie, Noël Coward, Ronald Colman, Charles Boyer, Red Skelton.

47. THE MONTE CARLO STORY. United Artists, 1957. (c) *Samuel A. Taylor*. Sp: Samuel A. Taylor, b/o story by Marcello Girosi and Dino Risi. Cast: Vittorio De Sica, Arthur O'Connell, Natalie Trundy, Jane Rose, Mischa Auer, Renato Rascel.

48. WITNESS FOR THE PROSECUTION. United Artists, 1957. *Billy Wilder*. Sp: Billy Wilder and Harry Kurnitz b/o play by Agatha Christie. Cast: Charles Laughton, Tyrone Power, Elsa Lanchester, John Williams, Henry Daniell, Ian Wolfe, Una O'Connor, Torin Thatcher, Norma Varden, Francis Compton.

49. TOUCH OF EVIL. Universal-International, 1958. *Orson Welles*. Sp: Orson Welles, b/o novel *Badge of Evil* by Whit Masterson. Cast: Orson Welles, Charlton Heston, Janet Leigh, Akim Tamiroff, Joseph Calleia, Ray Collins, Joanna Moore, Dennis Weaver, Valentin De Vargas, Mort Mills, Mercedes McCambridge, Joseph Cotten.

50. JUDGMENT AT NUREMBERG. United Artists, 1961. *Stanley Kramer*. Sp: Abby Mann. Cast: Spencer Tracy, Burt Lancaster, Richard Widmark, Maximilian Schell, Judy Garland, Montgomery Clift, William Shatner, Edward Binns, Werner Klemperer.

51. THE BLACK FOX. Heritage, 1962. *Louis Clyde Stoumen*. Sp: Louis Clyde Stoumen. Dietrich narrated this documentary film.

52. PARIS WHEN IT SIZZLES. Paramount, 1964. (c) *Richard Quine*. Sp: George Axelrod, b/o story by Julien Duvivier and Henri Jeanson. Cast: Audrey Hepburn, William Holden, Noël Coward. Dietrich had walk-on.

INDEX

158

ABOUT

Charle   lern Art. He
prepar   Elia Kazan
(1971   *nt*, and he
has al   *k*, and *The
Villag*

ABOUT